I AM THE NEW BLACK

TRACY MORGAN
I AM THE NEW BLACK

WITH
ANTHONY
BOZZA

SPIEGEL & GRAU
NEW YORK
2009

Copyright © 2009 by Street Life Productions, Inc.

All rights reserved.

Published in the United States by Spiegel & Grau,
an imprint of The Random House Publishing Group,
a division of Random House, Inc., New York.

SPIEGEL & GRAU and Design is a registered
trademark of Random House, Inc.

Photo credits can be found on page 197.

LIBRARY OF CONGRESS CATALOGING-IN-PUBLICATION DATA

Morgan, Tracy.
I am the new black/Tracy Morgan.
p. cm.
ISBN 978-0-385-52777-4
1. Morgan, Tracy. 2. Comedians—United States—Biography.
3. African American comedians—Biography. 4. Actors—United
States—Biography. 5. African American actors—Biography. I. Title.
PN2287.M6998A3   2009
792.7'6028092—dc22   2009032086
[B]

Printed in the United States of America on acid-free paper

www.spiegelandgrau.com

9 8 7 6 5 4 3 2 1

FIRST EDITION

Book design by Casey Hampton

For my mother and my father

CONTENTS

There are many reasons why you might be reading this sentence. You're obviously curious about me, or you wouldn't even be holding this book. That's cool with me, I'm happy about that, Mr. or Mrs. Whoever You Are. If there's one thing I've learned in my life, it's that curiosity might kill cats, but it doesn't kill people. Unless you're curious about doing things like bungee jumping high on crack to see if you really need that harness, curiosity will not kill you! I tell you what will kill you—people will. We've got a long way to go to change that around, but I hope we do. For now, I can say this and I know it's true: Curiosity makes you smarter. Don't fight it! Learn to learn, learn to ask questions. Clearly, you've got questions about me. In this book you'll find some answers.

I have a pretty diverse audience, and that makes me happy—laughter is universal, and I don't differentiate between people at all. Why should I? People are people. There's no reason why one person can't relate to any other person on this planet in some way or another. That's something I didn't have to be taught—I believed that as a kid, and leading the crazy life I've led has done nothing but prove me right to myself. I have friends who are black, white, purple, gay, straight, Martian, yellow, old, and young. I have friends who are animals and a few who I believe to be robots. All of them are people to me. In my mind it's not about what you look like or what you do, it's about who you are *inside*.

I hope whoever you are inside likes surprises, because I've got a few in store for you here. I'm not a child star, but you could say that I've grown up on TV. I went from being an unknown, down-and-out comic from Brooklyn and the Bronx to being a regular character on a major network comedy called *Martin*. From there I went on to become the most notable black comic on *Saturday Night Live* since Eddie Murphy. Then I had my own show, *The Tracy Morgan Show,* and now I'm on *30 Rock*. I definitely went from a boy to a man on TV, *all* on NBC—what up, Lorne Michaels! But here's what you don't know: I was already a man of the streets. I had to be to survive my upbringing.

The version of me you see on TV now and in my feature films is a pretty happy guy, isn't he? Finally, in my personal life, that much is true too—or it's getting there. Happiness, contentment, security—that's all new for me. I've reached my forties and I can finally say that no one except me can take my house away from me. No one but me can put me on the street. But it wasn't always like that. My life growing up was a twisted Bronx version of *The Color Purple*. It had a much different soundtrack and no trees, but that desperation was the *same*. At this point in my life I plan for the future. Back then I planned how to get through one day at a time.

Let me make one thing clear right now: I'm not writing this for your sympathy, and I don't feel like any kind of hero. I'm not God's gift, but my life wasn't dumb luck either. As you'll see, I made a series of choices—some bad, most good—that led me here. I don't want your praise, but I do want to be an example. Not the kind of example the principal suspends for throwing food at the teacher or the cops arrest in front of his friends for spray painting EAT MY ASS on the school. I want to be an example of a guy who made something of himself out of nothing. A guy who overcame the odds of a tough childhood, who worked hard, who didn't let his surroundings get the best of him and lead him to jail or the graveyard. Where I ended up—being a comedian, a TV star, and a movie actor—might be unique but my story is not. When a child is born, it's born with a heart of gold, but the way of this world can turn that heart cold. I'm still a good person and I thank God for that—He's working with me on it.

In many ways, all of you reading this who are like me, who come from what I came from—we are the last of the Mohicans. I've seen so many of the black males I grew up with end up dead or in prison. My closest friends from school who are still living work with me or for me, and I'm not exaggerating when I say that we are all that's left from our old crew. I keep them close because they're the only people I trust.

We grew up in the inner city, New York, in the late seventies and early eighties. We saw the birth of hip-hop right on our front stoop. Those were the good times; we were poor, but for a while there was harmony in our community. And those of us whose homes weren't what they should have been found what we needed in the neighborhood, because back then there were role models to be had. Hanging out on corners wasn't always dangerous—they weren't always just places to sell drugs. Back in my day, generations of families would meet on the street just to be together. Kids like me, from broken homes, used to be able to find family just outside their door, among a network of neighbors. We were all brothers of other mothers back when I was young. But not for long.

As we became teenagers, all of that slipped away. The city turned its back on the Bronx and let the neighborhoods become hoods, fueled by drugs. My backyard became the city's market for crack and heroin, and our people were right there to participate in every way—as dealers, as addicts, and as statistics day after day. Throughout the eighties and into the nineties, my high school friends and cousins were taken down by drug-related violence. My own family was no different. We were torn apart by drugs and AIDS. I lost a lot of role models to that terrible twosome: dirty needles and a disease society didn't understand. Like a lot of the young men in my neighborhood, I ended up on the streets dealing just to get by. We dropped like dominoes, pushed over by the end of a gun or the tip of a needle.

If you think about it, I really shouldn't be here at all. If you're the kind of person who likes numbers and statistics, I'm the long shot, the lotto Powerball winner. I'm the mutation in the DNA that makes evolution a reality. I am the new black. Once you know a little bit more of my story, you'll probably agree that the odds were against me sitting in a luxury apartment in Manhattan starring in an Emmy-winning series with an Emmy nomination myself, alongside people like Tina Fey and Alec Baldwin on a network like NBC. Given the facts of my life, those of you who like to spend time at the OTB would have put your money on finding me, at my age, curled up in a ball in a corner of the ghetto ready to die if I wasn't dead already. The Emmy nod surprised me: I thought they'd wait a few years to give this black man his trophy. I figured I'd just keep rocking the Golden Globes. I love you, Europe!

I'm not going to lie: I know I've got a natural talent that has seen me through my trials and tribulations. Being funny has been my bulletproof vest. This mouth of mine and my goofy face have kept me from getting shot many times, particularly that one time when I stole a drug dealer's girl. Being funny wasn't a career choice growing up, it was my way out of situations, a way to survive another day. In the end, it also freed me from my environment. It was my passport to a larger world that I had no idea existed, even though it was just a few miles south in Manhattan. That world was in the same city, in the same country, a world so many people took for granted, but it was foreign to a guy like me. When I finally moved to a nice community in Riverdale from a run-down apartment next to Yankee Stadium in the Bronx, it was like I'd landed on Mars. I had no idea that other people lived without garbage all over their streets. It's crazy to me how in America different people can live just a few miles away from each other but entire worlds apart.

The best thing that ever happened to me was being brought up hard. It's kept me hungry, even though now I've got more than I ever thought I'd see in this lifetime. It doesn't matter how much I accumulate—I'll be starving for the rest of my life, that's for damn sure. They say when opportunity knocks you should let it in and invite it to sit at your table. Fuck that—when opportunity knocks, you should take it *captive*. Beat that shit *down*. I've got opportunity tied to a chair in my basement with a ball gag in its mouth. Opportunity ain't even thinking about leaving my house. If you keep quiet for a second, you'll hear it whining.

But success isn't everything. Success can be tough if where you're from can't coexist with where you're at, if you know what I mean. If you don't know what I mean, let me break it down. As Biggie said, "Mo' money, mo' problems," and he was right. He was a big fat genius. When you're on top, it's amazing how many old friends you have! People like to push your buttons a little too much: Either they want you to perform for them or they want your money, and they'll take what they want one way or another. My sense of humor is my gift, and I need to protect it, whatever it takes. So I stay out of the street. It makes me sad, but at this point in my life, I can't go back and hang out where I used to live. I cannot have the kinds of negative energy I find there around me. And more than ever, I stay away from people I don't know. Most motherfuckers are miserable, and misery loves company. Fuck that—misery makes its own company if there's no company around. Misery is a crowd.

The truth is, I've never thought of myself as the Michael Jordan of comedy. And that's a good thing. You know why? Because I'm not. Wasn't that Richard Pryor? Yes, it was. I know what I am: I'm funny! As far as funny goes, I've got *big* funny! But take it from me because I should know: There's a Tracy Morgan on every block in every neighborhood like the one I came from— that kid who's off-the-wall funny, who takes on characters for any situation, who can entertain you when the shit is going down. Entertaining people is how he gets through life, and watching him live out loud like that makes your day better. At least he hopes so. That guy was me. That guy *is* me. I'm tough like a rock, and here I am, against all odds, still going strong in your hands and on your TV.

If you know that kid, or, better yet, if you *are* that kid, I hope that you get out of this book all that I put into it. I hope you're brave enough to be yourself, however different or strange you are. Most of all, I hope you avoid all the wolves and the pitfalls that surround you. If you're born into a situation you didn't ask for, where everything and everyone around you tells you that the easiest thing to do is to fall in line, to follow the crowd straight

into danger or a dead end, trust your inner strength. Don't do it.
There is always a way out.

It will be a lot of work, believe me. You need to pray to whatever god you believe in for help. And I'm not gonna lie to you: If and when you get what you want, the struggle doesn't end, because once you're free, there is always someone there waiting to drag you down if you let them. But if you don't let them and you achieve the goal you set for yourself, however big or small, there is nothing better. That is freedom on your own terms. Some people out there probably think I know nothing, but believe me, that is one truth I know. Because I'm living it.

If you're wondering what the title of my book might mean, well, before we get started, I'm gonna tell you. I don't mean to speak for all black Americans, and I don't think I am the evolution of my race or anything. Black people might be proud of their own, but if I was ever so arrogant as to say something like that and mean it, I might go down in history as the first black man lynched by black people. And speaking of lynching, I hope you all know that racism is alive and well in this country. Alive and living, I tell you.

Whenever a black comedian achieves a certain level of success, they get asked about racism in the entertainment industry. Every time I see or hear a question like that I think of a joke Damon Wayans did in his stand-up back when he really blew up and earned something like $14 million in a year for the first time. Damon's joke went something like this:

Reporters have been asking me, "Damon, now that you have this $14 million, do you think racism still exists?" And I tell them, while I'm counting my money, "Well if'n there is any, suh, I ain't seen none!"

The new black is impossible to define—and so am I, because I am the new black. You know my characters on television and in films, and some of you know my stand-up. Which one of those is me? Who am I? Tracy Jordan? Biscuit? Astronaut Jones? The truth is that I'm all of them. They all live in me and I live through all of them. If you want to know the truth about Tracy Morgan, that truth is that like the new black, I'm impossible to define. Black isn't the absence of color, it's the presence of all colors. That's why I'm the new black. I'm everyone you've seen me be and just myself at the same time.

We are in a new era, with a black president. Racism definitely still exists, and the new black knows this, just like the new black knows that now is the time to stand up. The new black is something that our American society needs at every level, because the new black isn't about race, it's about *trying*. In this era of the new black, you have to try because there's no more excuses. We've got to take responsibility. We've got to raise our children. And people! This book is going to take your excuses from you. If I could get to where I am from where I came from, so can you. Being the new black means you can get there if you try. No more excuses. If your life is hard, you gotta start laughing so you don't cry, and you've gotta try or you'll get nothing. We can make a change if we put in the work.

Okay, okay, I've gotta stop this train. I'm not about to jump up on a soapbox blaming society and the economy and the white-man government of the United States for all of the hardships in my life (you bastards already know what you did). Seriously, hasn't all that been said already? Don't we all know that shit by now? We do, right? If any of you don't, let me point you to the Interwebs or your local public library, where you'll find nice search engines or sweet ladies with glasses to help you find material to read.

I'm here to relate my personal experience, because growing up in the inner city as a child of the seventies is a state of mind and a state of being. I am a product of those times, and like many others, I've struggled to get past them. There's no one to blame for the bad habits I brought with me when I left the ghetto, though. I almost let them ruin me. Even though now I see them for what they are, they're never dead and buried. They're a part of me just like the parts that make you laugh when you see me on TV. No one's demons ever die; if you're strong, they stay caged and you become their warden. That's where I'm at. I fight my demons every day, and I've gotten to know them so well, they've got a name: Chico Divine. You'll meet Chico in a little while; he's the life of the party whose ass I still got to bury every morning.

In my opinion, life don't come easy no matter who you are. These past forty years have been crazy, but everything I did was worth it, and I'm nothing but grateful to be here now. Would I do it all again? Stupid question! I've got my health, which is much better now than it used to be, even though I've got diabetes. Sure, I've had a lot of complications from it for someone my age, but I still feel lucky—growing up with a complete ignorance of nutrition, I'd be dead by now if I'd never found a way out of the Bronx. I consider my health a blessing. What else do I have? I've got a career I wouldn't trade for anything. I've got opportunity locked in my basement. I've got three great kids. I've got cars, all that stupid shit. I had a great marriage; after twenty years we split up, but we're still friends. I've a girlfriend who is good to me, and there is no shortage of women I'd like to get pregnant.

And I've got a future now too. That's the one thing I never considered back in Brooklyn in 1975. I've got something to live for past the end of the day, past the end of the week, and past the bills due on the first of the month. As a young man, I expected none of that. As a full-grown man, I appreciate all of it. Even at my craziest, when I forgot all about drinking and driving being illegal and dangerous, I didn't overlook any of those hard-earned privileges.

I hope you're interested in hearing the story of my life, because now that we've talked for a bit, I'm ready to get down to it. Some of the situations you are gonna read about may be pretty regular stuff to some of you, and some of the bullshit, to whatever degree, is probably all too familiar to most of you. Everyone else should know that this story is not all good. There's not a big happy ending waiting for you, rubbed down in oil on a beach in Miami.

Sure there's happiness, if you need to know now. Yeah, I'm a success and I am happy. But the only one celebrating at my party right now is me. As of this moment, I'm estranged from my own mother and most of my family, and I'm not sure that's going to change much. I'm not saying why, I'm just saying that's how it is. It's okay though. I've gotten used to it. I'm an island, kind of like Antigua: hot and humid, definitely a destination of choice if you want to get freaky or just kick back. And pretty isolated.

If there's one thing I hope you take away from your visit to my world, whether you care to read about all I've lived or whether you stop right here, it's this: There are two things that will get you through life, and those things are simple and human and anyone can have them. They're laughter and learning. If they're a part of your life, you will always have a reason to keep living. If anyone out there has found a better way to make this world a better place to be, lay it on me, I'm here. Speak up, because I'm always listening and I'm always eager to learn.

I AM THE NEW BLACK

CHAPTER 1

Roots

Every good story I know starts at the very beginning, because like that white lady said in *The Sound of Music,* it's a very good place to start. My story doesn't start the day I was born, because that isn't the very beginning. My story starts years before I was born.

In the 1950s, America decided it was a good idea to try to fight communism in tropical jungles on other side of the world. When JFK was president, he seemed to think we needed to help the Vietnamese, but that ultimately they would need to figure themselves out on their own. Once he died, Lyndon Johnson took office and became the guy who really made a big national issue out of it for us. President Johnson and his administration, in their infinite wisdom, tripled our military presence in Vietnam, basically upping the ante on some crazy idea of President Eisenhower's from about ten years before. I don't understand how anyone can like Ike.

Shouldn't our presidents be given tests for common sense? I'm no military strategist, but I think the people in power from the late fifties through to the seventies were a bunch of paranoid white dudes. In the way that the PTA looks at marijuana as the gateway drug, those guys thought of 'Nam as the gateway to worldwide communism. They told the American people, who at first really bought into this shit, that if we let those communist Russians get stoned on Vietnam, they'd become addicted to takeover. Soon they'd be selling their crackhead philosophy all across Asia and into Europe. Then they'd hook up with their homey Castro in Cuba and have a huge commie cartel poisoning our free democratic minds in America. There'd go the whole damn neighborhood. The Russians were supposed to be some kind of new Hitler, and if we didn't get that communism out of 'Nam, we'd be eating Kremlin Nuggets in McDonald's over here in no time.

That was how they sold it. I still think it's crazy. The Russians lived thousands of miles away, where it snowed and they drank vodka and ate potatoes and waited on line for toilet paper all day. They had their ideals, and Lenin and Marx were like their Biggie and Tupac, but I don't think those guys gave a fuck about Vietnam, or at least not nearly as much as we thought they did. It would be like New York and L.A. fighting over Ohio in the East Coast/West Coast rap wars. Can you see that happening? What the hell could either side want with Ohio? A parking lot for their Bentleys?

In the end, our government sent eight million of our young men—that's an entire generation—over to Southeast Asia to serve, and hundreds of thousands came back dead or wounded or too fucked up to live right. We don't have much else to show for it, so if you ask me, everything about that war was just *wrong*. It wasn't the kind of war we could win because there wasn't anything really to fight for! You'd think that after that kind of a blow to America's self-esteem, presidents would be more careful about invading places with complicated histories. Apparently, dudes from Texas whose fathers were president don't learn lessons like that. Anyone who knows anything about Vietnam wouldn't have wasted our country's time and money and lives in Iraq because it's the same kind of war, just this time in a desert. Listen, I wasn't much of a student, but there's one thing I took away from U.S. history class: An army of stuffy British redcoats couldn't beat a bunch of hick farmers with holes in their boots because they were fighting in the farmers' own backyards! Was Bush not a baseball fan? Doesn't he know about the home-field advantage? You can't ignore that shit! Ask any cop who's tried to run down a crack-head in his own hood—nine out of ten times, the crackhead won't get caught. He's got the home/hood advantage.

Let me get back to my point, which is that my dad, Jimmy, was one of so many young men who went to Vietnam. He was drafted in 1965 and served four or five tours. Unlike a lot of his friends who went alongside him, he managed to make it back in one piece, physically at least. But just like other survivors, he was torn to pieces inside by what he'd seen and what he'd had to do to survive. My dad was taken from me when I was a teenager, so I didn't get the chance to speak to him man to man about what he lived through, but I got a sense of it from the stories he told.

He tried to always end those stories with something cheerful, because that was the way he looked at life, but you could hear the hardship through it anyway. When my dad would tell me about hard days and sleepless nights in the jungle, he'd spend more time talking about his friends telling jokes and singing Motown songs to get through it together. But one time when I was in high school, he sat me down and really leveled with me. He told me that he'd been a helicopter gunner and that countless times he killed people that he didn't know. He'd watch them fall to the ground hundreds of feet below him every time he pulled that trigger.

"It was war," he said to me, without a smile on his face. "It was bloody."

He got real quiet and I couldn't think of anything to say. He was my hero, and I was just trying to picture him, not much older than I was at the time, in a helicopter above a jungle, leaning out the door shooting people every day, just to stay alive.

"I never told you who you're named after, did I, Tray?"

That wasn't what I was expecting to hear. "No, Dad. You and Mom said you just liked the way it sounded."

"Well, we did, but there's more to it," he said.

When my dad got on that army transport plane leaving America headed to Vietnam, he spent the next twenty-four hours or however long it took to get over there sitting next to an Irish guy named Tracy. They were the same age and came from very different backgrounds, but they became real close, considering the circumstances. They talked about all that they were leaving behind and all that they were going to face. They talked about being scared and how long they thought this war would go on. He said he knew that guy better after one day with him than he did members of his own family. They landed and got their assignments, and the next day my dad's new friend Tracy was dead. He was all in pieces because he stepped on a land mine. He was going home in a body bag after one day in the shit.

"That taught me everything I needed to know about the war," my dad said. "I never forgot that time I spent with him, because all that talking we did put me at ease. I figured that we'd be friends forever, but that's how war is. And that's how you got your name."

I was sad to hear that story but glad too. Because let's face it—Tracy Morgan? That's an Irish female's name. With a name like that, I should have red hair, blue eyes, and big titties. I should be in a green bikini on a float every March.

When I think of Vietnam or see it referenced in a movie or a script, the first image that comes to mind is my father in his field uniform, fighting in that jungle. As an older man, when I've been faced with challenges, I remember that at seventeen my father went to fight a war on the other side of the world. I look at my girlfriend, Taneisha, whose brother was sent to fight in Iraq. He left home at eighteen. I wonder what he was thinking about as he flew over there. I wonder if his experience was similar to my dad's.

Taneisha told me that her brother slept as much as he could on his way to war. He didn't want to think about it. He tried to avoid it by sleeping, but he couldn't hide from it: On one of his first days there he saw a baby who had been shot in the head lying on the side of the road. Her brother is back home, thank God, but that is the kind of stuff that he can never forget. He had a hard time readjusting, but he got through it. He goes to church five days a week now.

When I was a kid I'd wake up at night and find my dad walking around the house, patrolling. I'd be on my way to the bathroom and I'd ask him, "Dad, are you all right?" And he'd just stare at me. I don't even know if he knew I was there. He was just in his head, still patrolling, still in Vietnam. He couldn't shake it. I used to break down crying about that, even as a young kid, because I knew at those moments that I'd never have my dad. I could never have my father in his entirety because a huge part of him was never going to be there.

My dad spent a good chunk of his youth in a strange land full of swamps, rice paddies, and mountains, watching villages get burned and children get killed and families get wiped out. He saw his friends from the neighborhood and the friends he made in the army gunned down before his eyes. Every day he fought to survive more than he fought an enemy he could identify. My father wasn't a violent man. He was a musician. He went to Vietnam a boy and came back a man, a very different man than he would have become otherwise. He came back with memories and bad habits that he couldn't shake for a long time. *That* is the heart and soul of my story, and that is where my very beginning is. It's not a very good place to start. You hear me, Julie Andrews? I learned how to be a man from my father, and because of what his life had done to him, I learned a few other things too. I think I'm just now trying to unlearn some of those lessons or at least see them for what they are—the good, the bad, the all of it. All of the humanity of where I'm coming from has only just become clear to me.

What I'm saying is that my father picked up bad habits over there just like I picked up bad habits in show business. Show business is my Vietnam and this life is the war that I'm fighting. We've all got our wars. We're all victims of our battles because in war nobody wins. My father? The only thing that kept him sane was his music, but he died paying the price for his sins anyway.

My father, Jimmy junior, was the oldest child of Jimmy Morgan, Sr., and Roselle Morgan. After him came Macy, Pat, Alvin, Cynthia, and Lorraine; there were six of them. Two of them are already dead—both of the boys died of AIDS that they caught from shooting up with dirty needles. The girls are widows, except for one. There was always music around their house because the Morgans were very religious and sang in the church choir. From a young age, my father showed real talent as a musician. He played piano and keyboards, and he was good. Entirely self-taught, he never knew how to read music, but he could figure out a synthesizer without any manual, that's for sure. My dad was a leader; when he was in bands after the war, he was always the leader, no matter what kind of band it was. I know in my heart that I get my leadership qualities from him, because all I ever saw him do was arrange everything for everyone around him. That's why I am the way I am. I make sure the people around me have what they need. I saw my dad always yelling at motherfuckers about being late to rehearsal, and I'm the same way if someone on my ship don't toe the line. My father wrote all the music his bands played; he booked the shows, dealt with the club owners and all that. I saw real quick that if there was something I wanted to make happen, I should learn to do it all myself.

My mother's and father's families lived in the same projects— the Tompkins Houses on Tompkins and Myrtle Avenue in the Bedford-Stuyvesant section of Brooklyn. My father's family lived in apartment 12M, and my mother's lived in 14M. My best friend, Allen, he lived in 13M. It was like one big house—those apartments were right on top of one another, and we ruled those three floors. It was our place on that end of those hallways. We were all poor, but back then life was good out there. Neighbors looked out for each other. It's not like that now because it's all violent and people are only looking for what they can take from each other, not how they can help. But I grew up there in a time when things were a little bit different.

My mother's parents were Dave and Alice Warden, and my mother was the second-oldest in her family, after her sister Patricia, my aunt Pat. She was followed by my uncle Dave, my aunt Brenda, my aunt Robin, my uncle Michael, then my aunt

Michelle, who died when she was still a baby, and finally my aunt Kim—a family of eight. Their family was quite different from my dad's because they were Jehovah's Witnesses. Not my mother's father—he never went to meetings or church—but my grandmother and a few of my mom's sisters were very into it. Her family was kind and loving, but strict and very, very straightlaced.

My father's parents' home was definitely a looser place to be, with people laughing and hanging around and playing music, while the Wardens' home was like church on Sunday—every day. But I loved it there too. My mom's mother, Alice, was my baby. She was my heart. She was the one who gave me the love. Grandma Alice was more affectionate to me than anyone else was, my parents included. She'd hug me, she'd kiss me, and give me all the attention I really needed as a kid. She died a year before my father did, back when I was in high school, and I was devastated. I was living with my dad up in the Bronx at the time, and I remember coming home from school that day and him telling me she'd died. I broke down right there. And as soon as I got myself together I took the train out to Brooklyn. I had to be in her place with my mom's family right away. Alice Warden was my baby. I dedicated every single race I ran in track and every football game I played to her for the rest of my high school sports career. She was my surrogate mom during the years my mother and I didn't see eye to eye.

My parents met each other just hanging out in that tight little community of their building. They fell in love young and they got started young, just before my dad went off to war. I should be clear about this—they got *busy* before my father went off to war. That's what I mean when I say they got *started*. My dad had this habit of getting my mother pregnant every time he was out the door to the army again. Can you blame a motherfucker? I'd make sure I got as much pussy as possible before I headed off to hell. My dad had his priorities straight.

His children are all the evidence you need to see that I'm not lying. My brother Jimmy was born in 1966, while my dad was away on his first tour. My dad came back, was stationed at a base in New York, and before he was redeployed he went AWOL, ran his ass out to Brooklyn, grabbed my mother by the ass, and made me. A day or two later the MPs showed up and found him, took him away, and off he went again to Vietnam. Now, here's the kind of man my dad was: Later on in life, when I was a teenager, he walked me past the bleachers where I was conceived. That's right. We went to a family reunion at some relative's place out in East New York, and my dad took me for a man-to-man walk. I always liked those moments with him because Jimmy Morgan might have died young, but he was an old soul, full of wisdom. So I'm strolling with him and we're talking and I'm wondering where we're going. I'm waiting for him to drop some science.

"I'm going to show you something," he said as we walked onto the field at the local high school.

I was expecting some kind of inspirational pep talk about track or football, because those were the only things I cared about at the time. I thought maybe he was going to tell me about a great winning moment or a memorable game or something. I was definitely hanging on his every word.

He stopped in front of a set of metal bleachers at the side of the field. "You see these, son?" he asked.

"Yeah, Dad."

"This is where I busted a nut inside your mother and made you," he said.

"Oh yeah?"

"We were right under here. I had your mother doggy-style

and gave it to her *good* too. You came right out of me right here under these stands, little man."

"Dad?"

"Yeah, son?"

"I really didn't need to know that shit."

"Well, it's true. A man should know his roots."

My dad taught me how to tell a story. He always brought an unforgettable detail.

Nine months after my parents had sex under the bleachers, on November 10, 1968, I came into the world. The next time my dad was back from Nam, they made my sister, Asia, who was born in 1970, and then my brother Paris, who was born in 1972. It was like clockwork with them, but how could it not be with him always going off and maybe never coming back? It was that now-or-never sex. There's people out there who know what I'm talking about. All you girls who gave a little more than you thought you would because you knew you might never see that man again? You know who you are. All of us in show business or with a little money and a busy schedule know you too. And you should believe us when we tell you that we love you. Because we do.

My father came home in 1975, when the war was over. By that time I was six and very eager to know him. He did his best to fall back into a normal life with my mother and Jim, Asia, Paris, and me, which meant trying to handle privately the worst thing he brought home with him—a heroin problem he couldn't shake. I'm not going to make excuses for him because I was never old enough or mature enough to talk to him seriously about his addiction, but I know that he picked up the habit in Vietnam, and I feel okay saying that I understand how that might have happened. If I woke up every day not knowing how much longer I'd be alive, I'd look for something to numb me out and calm me down. I'm not excusing anything, but I don't hate the man for doing what he had to do to get by. Hate the game, not the player.

I need to take a minute to say this now: Our soldiers in Iraq are coming back damaged in a similar way. It's already happening. If you check your local news, you'll see that some of the first vets to return from Iraq have committed crimes or committed suicide. These young people need help, and I hope that the government has learned a lesson from the Vietnam experience about what happens when our troops come home. We can't expect fucked-up motherfuckers to come back from the front lines and just fit in, generation after generation. Compassion is only the beginning of what they need. Those guys need *help*. When my dad came back, no one wanted to hear about what happened to those boys in Vietnam because it ruined the spirit of America. All them rich kids who got to protest the war and take acid and listen to Jimi Hendrix and enjoy all the free love—they forgot something very important while they were seeing their friends' heads turn into giant yellow submarines: Most of the poor young men like my dad who went over there and served didn't ask to go. But to the hippie nation that my dad returned to, everything and everyone related to the war was wrong. Once it was over, no one wanted to talk about it, no matter what side they'd been on. Vietnam was like a big girl everybody in the hood had been with but no one greeted on the street. Vietnam was a fat girl with gonorrhea; it was an embarrassment that nobody in America would be able to forget. Society asked those soldiers to suffer things they couldn't handle, all alone, in silence, because society couldn't handle the aftermath.

Not long after my dad returned for good, my parents split up, so my memories of what their marriage was really like aren't all that clear. I know that the one thing that gave him happiness was playing music, and he worked hard to put bands together and make money by spreading some joy that way. Like I said before, my father was a born leader. He was a natural for that role because he was funny—he could get anyone to follow his lead or stop fighting and work together. His sense of humor was disarming in the same way that Richard Pryor's was. He was great at sizing up a situation and talking about the things that no one else in the room was going to mention but everyone knew were there. And he did it by making them all smile. Jimmy Morgan . . . man, he was dynamite.

The music he wrote was dynamite too. It was pure R & B, like Rick James and Prince, with a touch of Jimi Hendrix. And he always had great band names: 100% Pure was one; Tuff was another. When I was sixteen, I was his roadie and traveled with him all summer. We toured down the East Coast into the Carolinas, his band playing these little blues clubs. And hands down, my dad was the funniest man on the bus.

This was quite a few years after my parents split up. I was young when he got home from the army, but even I could tell something was wrong. The heroin and the post-traumatic stress ate him up inside and took him further away from my mother and us kids every day. He really couldn't keep it together, and even though my mother loved him, it got to the point where she just couldn't have the drugs around her babies. One time she came home and found my little brother crawling around in his room playing with a needle, and that was that. She kicked my father out that day. They loved each other though, and that breakup wasn't final. They tried to make it work after that. He had to stay somewhere else when he wasn't clean, but when he was, he would move back in with us. She kept hoping they could work it out, but he couldn't kick the shit cold turkey. It took him a few years to get off it.

I remember how upset my mother would be when my dad wouldn't come home. At the time we were living in Coney Island in the Marlboro Houses, apartment 2 on the first floor. It was bad when my dad was gone, but it was worse when he was home. He had these intense nightmares and screamed so loud that he woke up our whole household and sometimes our neighbors too. I remember being in bed next to my brother, both of us crying because Daddy was screaming so loud. We'd hear my mother trying to wake him, talking to him, calling his name, but he wouldn't stop. Our neighbors would knock on the door, and one time they actually came in to try to help, but there was nothing anyone could do. They'd shake my dad. They'd shout, "Jimmy! Jimmy! You're okay! You're here! You're in bed with your wife! You're okay! Jimmy, you're safe!" It didn't help. He'd keep on yelling until whatever horror he was reliving in his dreams finally faded away.

The night terrors were bad enough; with the drugs on top of that, my mother couldn't take it anymore, and once she decided to get her kids out, she moved us back to Tompkins Houses to be near my grandparents. We had an apartment a few floors up from both her folks and my dad's. I didn't see my father for a time after that, but slowly, as he started to get the drugs out of his life, my mother let us see him more often. She was always cool about that. She wanted us to know our dad. Once she was convinced that he was clean and fit to watch us, she would let us spend weekends with him. The two of them couldn't work out their differences, and after a while it became clear that they'd never get back together. That was hard, but at least we were seeing my dad. It got stranger when my mom and dad started dating other people. But the hardest part was not having my dad around me every day as I got older. As a grown man with sons of my own, there's one thing I know for sure: A growing boy *needs* his dad.

In the black community there's a saying: We raise our daughters but we love our sons. The girls are brought up to make money and get by, and the boys are spoiled. I need every black baby daddy out there to listen to me: That shit has got to change. It's old, man. All you single fathers got to man up. Nothing will ever change for black people in America if men don't realize that no boy can become a man if he doesn't have a dad. I don't care that we have a black president now; it doesn't mean things are going to change for black people. We all need to be the change. Every black man has got to realize that if he's man enough to make a son, he'd better damn well be ready to be a dad. If you're not a leader, leave the condom on! It only takes one night to become one, but it takes a lifetime to *be* one. It takes sperm to be a father, but it takes a heart to be a dad. That's something I can take to the grave—no matter what I've done in life, I've always done right by my kids. All you young men out there, you have to trust me. If you take responsibility for your actions, you will truly be free, knowing you've done the right thing and played the most important role a man can ever play in this thing we call life.

When I was nine or ten, after my parents were living apart, my mother started seeing a guy named Sonny. Right away, I didn't like him. When I got older, I realized why: because he was fucking my mother! It's simple. Sonny, who was not my father, was fucking my mother. Until he showed up, I always thought that my mom and dad were going to get back together. I thought they were just taking a vacation from each other. To me, it was just a matter of time before we were all under one roof again. When you're nine, you don't understand what sex is. Sex is just what makes babies, so only your mom and dad should be having sex because they made you and your brothers and sisters.

That's where my head was at after nine years.

Of course, when I got older I became a motherfucker myself so I understood what Sonny was up to hanging around my mom. There was only one reason Sonny was showing up at our door with bags of food and presents: He wanted to fuck her! I was distracted by the food and the presents—that's why he brought them—but I still knew some shit wasn't right. I was like a dog smelling rotten meat; I just kept doing little circles around Sonny, never taking a bite. Whenever he came over I knew we were gonna eat well, but I wasn't as happy about that as I should have been. Instead it made me angry. I was smelling something that was unfamiliar—the trading of groceries for pussy. Looking back, I don't fault my mother at all. She could have done a hell of a lot worse to put food on the table.

Sonny coming by was definitely an awakening for me though. I missed my dad. My older brother, Jim—I love him dearly—had contracted spinal meningitis as a child. By the time he was three years old, he was what anyone would call a cripple. His legs were basically useless. Jim Reality, as we call him, has always walked with two canes. It happened innocently enough. When he and my aunt Kim were little, they played with their toys in the toilet bowl like a lot of kids do, and they both got sick. My family brought them to the hospital. Kim was kept there for a few days, but my brother, the doctors said, was well enough to go home. Kim got better, but Jim got worse. He suffered nerve damage and lost the ability to walk. He and my mother filed a lawsuit that took about twenty years to process, but eventually they settled out of court and Jim got some money. And like you do when you get some money and you live in the ghetto, his family and my mom moved far away, right away. To Ohio. He had to get his family out of the way of danger, because everyone knows what happens in a neighborhood like that when people think you have money. I did the same thing when I got my first check from *Saturday Night Live*. I'm not joking when I tell you that people in the ghetto think that if you're on TV you have a million dollars and that you keep it in your house. They will come to your house to steal it, and they will kill you if that money is not there. And why would it be there? What is this, the 1800s? We have banks now! And debit cards!

By the time I was in ninth grade, Jim had undergone twenty-one surgeries. I was always there afterward to watch him, to help him out and to hold him when he'd cry out in pain as his body healed. I went with him to physical therapy and rehab all throughout our childhood. We were really close, and I was willing to do anything for him. In fact, once we got into high school, I ran track and played football as much for him as I did for me. He was always a sports fan, so I wanted him to feel like he was part of it, through me.

I learned the most important lesson in life from Jim: Nothing is a handicap unless you let it be. He's gone out there and done everything he ever wanted to do. He's full of life—one of the bravest people I've ever met. Even when we were kids, Jim never whined and never used his handicap to gain sympathy or any kind of advantage. He and I shared a room for years, until I left the house, and I never heard him complain or get mad at God or blame the world for his condition. He's my biggest hero for that reason—he understood his situation in this world right away, and instead of complaining or looking for the easy way out, he *adjusted*. And his attitude about it has never changed. "This is just the way it is supposed to be for me," he'll tell you, and give you a smile you won't forget. Whenever the stress I have to deal with makes me want to complain, I think of Jim. He keeps me humble; he's always right here in my heart. Thinking about how he

navigates life with his problems shuts me up about mine right away. After all, I can't feel too bad for Jim; his legs might not work, but he sure ain't paralyzed below the waist. Jim Reality's got eleven kids! Everything else on him works just fine.

Back on the playground when we were kids though, my older brother didn't play the same role as other kids' older brothers. He could kick some ass, and I saw him do it plenty of times, but he wasn't like this huge protector. I was definitely the kind of kid who invited trouble and got into fights, but I wasn't going to get out of trouble because my older brother could save me. Having a cripple for an older brother was like wearing a sign that said KICK MY ASS. Once some bully motherfuckers saw him coming over to back me up during a fight, they loved it. They thought they could kick my ass, Jim's ass, my sister's ass, and all our friends' asses, and just walk away free. They'd start laughing. "What the fuck?" they'd say. "You serious? I got to put this cripple to sleep too?"

That wasn't the case, because once Jim hobbled over to a kid, he could put him to sleep with one punch. Of course he could! He used his arms twice as much as the rest of us—all he needed was to land one punch. But that wasn't always going to happen, so to keep things from getting to that level, I learned to be funny. My brother and I could hold our own in fights when it came to it, but usually I diffused situations because I had perfected my skills at snaps. I made up "yo' mama" jokes for days because back then if you made everyone else laugh at the bully, no matter how big he was, that was better than knocking him out. At nine or ten years old, I started to realize that acting out and entertaining whoever was around had mad benefits. If I was the best class clown, I was safe, because being funny gave me power. Girls seemed to like it, and so did guys. And when someone wanted to hurt me, if I stood my ground and made him and everyone else around laugh, I could get myself out of any situation.

So I ran with funny from an early age, making jokes and acting crazy as much as I could. I took my humor as far as it could go, and there were a few times in my youth when I saw that sometimes funny can go too far. Like this one summer—I was eleven, I think—and someone at the public pool in our neighborhood stole my brand-new Pumas. At the time, there was not a damn thing in the world that I loved more than those sneakers. I was devastated—and mad as hell. But I didn't think about hunting the kid down or beating him up; I thought up a prank to get the thief back, and to make everyone else as mad as I was. Not very mature, but whatever, I was eleven.

I didn't know who stole my sneakers, but in my little boy detective's mind, I knew he was at the pool that day. Everyone I knew loved the pool, so I concluded that kid must love the pool too. There were so many kids there every day that I had no chance of finding him or my sneakers, so only one thing made sense to me. I had to get back at whoever it was by taking away something I knew he liked. I had to shut that pool *down*. Wasn't going to be any more swimming if I had no sneakers!

The next day, that pool was full of kids. In the middle of the afternoon the sun was blazing and everyone was enjoying the water. That's when I swam out into the middle of the pool and took a shit the size of a Milky Way. I made sure everyone saw it too. I pointed at it and started screaming like I had no idea where it came from.

They shut that place down like the beach in *Jaws* when them kids swim around with the fake fin! It was no joke, neither; that pool was so big that they had to drain it and treat it with chemicals, and by the time they got it going again, summer was almost over. Kids had nowhere to play for like a month, and it was hot that summer too. But I didn't care; someone stole my Pumas, so I stole their summer. If the party was over for *me,* the party was over for *everybody.* That's how I did it back when I was eleven.

I had gotten my revenge, but something else happened that I hadn't planned on. You see, I *liked* the feeling of shitting in that pool. This became a problem for me. I started shitting everywhere there was water after that. If I saw an open fire hydrant, I'd shit there. I had no shame—in the middle of the street, if water was flowing hard enough, I'd drop the brown shark. Our neighbors had a Slip 'n Slide—for one day. I shut that shit down. You should have seen what it looked like. I shat all up and down it, then slid all around in it and kept shitting. For like two years, I was the CEO of shutting down water on a summer day. I wasn't even a small child at that point, so it was sort of embarrassing. I am so glad I grew out of that. My hotel bills would be astronomical today.

It was pretty immature to drop brown bombs over a pair of sneakers, but that's where my mind was at. Once I got my first taste of pussy though, my focus changed. That was all I cared about, just pussy, girls, and getting more pussy. You've got to understand something: People in the hood are sexually active at an early age because everybody who is old enough is fucking! That's all you hear before you even know what it means—"This bitch is gonna suck my dick" or "I'm gonna fuck that nigger." There's not a whole lot else besides sex that will make you feel better when you've got nothing else in the world. So sex is all around you from the time you're a kid. You realize early on what your mom and dad and all the adults are doing because they can't get any privacy anyway. Apartments are small in the ghetto, and you think them walls keep out the sounds? Hell no! Everybody knows everybody's business because they can hear everything going on.

Where I'm from we played house a little bit different than a lot of you probably did. We knew by nine or ten that whoever was going to play the dad first was going to hump on the girl playing Mom. I'm not saying we went and had sex, but we were replicating what we saw, and the two kids playing the adults definitely went to "bed" and "Daddy" humped up and down on "Mommy" for a minute. Why do you think I'd fight with my brothers to play Daddy first? Sex is a funny thing—it's all hush-hush in the suburbs, but in the ghetto it's everywhere. That's the same reason white men can't dance. Black people dance well because we start early—there's music being played everywhere. White people? They don't start dancing until they get to college, and by then it's too late; the bottom don't move with the top no matter how hard they try. When I first moved to the suburbs I couldn't get over how silent it was every night. I got into all kinds of trouble for playing my stereo in my off-hours. And I was a full-grown man with a lucrative day job.

Anyway, by age eight, I was humping a pillow just about every night, playing house, getting what I could, until the summer just before my mom moved us out of the Marlboro Houses in Coney Island back to Tompkins. That's when I experienced real sex firsthand. I was eight and my brother Jim was ten, and we had a babysitter who gave us each a piece. Now, I know that might seem wrong and insane to a lot of you, but you got to understand what I'm saying: Where I'm from, and where a lot of people in this country are from, we play by another set of rules. Our babysitter was fourteen. My mom had dropped us off at her house, and no one else was there and this girl was horny and curious. The babysitter went and took a bath, and while she was in there she told my brother to come in and get on top of her. I watched him put his little ding-a-ling in her and after that I got on her and did the same. I don't count that as losing my virginity— I did that when I was twelve—but I guess it was. My brother liked it, but I didn't. I actually cried after that. I remember she gave me a stack of Oreo cookies to keep me quiet. It wasn't the only time it happened either. Damn. Memories.

Do you people know how *powerful* pussy is? That shit broke up the Beatles! Yoko Ono broke up the greatest rock-and-roll band ever! One piece of pussy ended it all. She walked into the studio and within a week she had John Lennon saying, "Ringo who? Paul what? We got some guy named George in this group? Fuck rehearsal, I'm banging it out with this Chinese bitch all day." That is what pussy can do. To quote Method Man: Nothing make a man feel better than a woman. And sometimes it becomes a problem.

That early experience was interesting I guess, but once I was twelve, I started bringing little girls my age up to my room to spend the night and keep my feet warm. And from then on I always had to have a piece of pussy around. Even when I was caught up in the middle of a divorce from my wife of twenty years, I felt no different. I still needed a bit of it handy. My divorce was the most traumatic change I've ever experienced—and I still thought about pussy as I was going through it. I've seen all kinds of death and I've had all kinds of health problems, but I can honestly tell you, no matter what was going on, my love for the ladies has never left me, not even for a minute.

I don't mean to just spit that out matter-of-factly, but I'm pretty desensitized to things that might be too much for people of a more protected upbringing to survive. I've seen too much to be shocked by anything. I know a man who has had a kid with a couple of sisters in the same family—that guy is my uncle! That guy is my mother's youngest brother, Michael Warden, who I call Uncle Fatty Love! I've seen people deal drugs at their kitchen table, right there in front of their little kids. I've heard about relatives robbing each other and killing each other over nothing, like it's no big deal. So my inappropriate babysitter is just another childhood memory to me.

Don't get me wrong: I'm desensitized but I'm not *insensitive*. I'm alive and thinking. I know where I'm from, and that knowledge, plus hard work and a lot of faith, are the reasons I'm here at all. That's my formula for success and the reason why you're reading this. It didn't hurt that I was given a gift and I realized it—my sense of humor. I learned how to put it out there to defend myself, and in return it came to save me. People ask me how I got so funny, and when I answer they get a strange look on their faces. I don't know what they want to hear—you think I got funny watching *The Little Rascals?* The truth is easy for me to say. I got funny for one reason: I got funny to *survive*.

CHAPTER 2

As Far As My Father Could Take Me
a.k.a. From a Boy to a Man

Being a teenager is like playing with nitroglycerine. By the time you're twelve or thirteen, you've got a mixture of adult and child on your hands, and it's pretty unstable. Subject it to excessive heat or pressure, and that thing's gonna explode. Even in an ideal life, it's hard to maintain balance when you consider the $x$factor of hormones.

When you're a teenager, you throw yourself out there to the world because it's calling for you. You don't care if the world is ready. The only thing that can hold you back is you. If you think you know everything, you might not survive being a teenager. I guarantee that you will think, for at least a year or three, that you know everything. Listen to me, teenagers—you don't! And acting like you do is nothing to be proud of. No matter how smart any of you teenagers think you are, you motherfuckers don't know shit! You have so much to learn it's *crazy*. I thought I knew it all, but I didn't know shit. I still didn't know shit well into my twenties and thirties! If I could bottle that teenage confidence and sell that musk, I'd make a fortune. When we're that age we think we're indestructible superheroes, like the Hulk. Teenagers think they can fly! But they can't. They can't even drive!

My friends and I were no different. The only proof we have about who was right and who was wrong today is which of us is still alive. There's one thing for sure when you grow up in the hood: Either you're gonna peak fast and burn out, or you're gonna figure yourself out and *survive*. If you don't choose, one of the two will happen to you whether you're ready for it or not. And I wouldn't count on being lucky; luck in the hood is like the seasons in Australia—that shit is the opposite of the rest of the world. Even if you just sit on the corner minding your own business, waiting for life to come to you, you might die just like the gangbanger who goes out looking for trouble every day. In the hood, sitting and waiting around as life goes by is just as much an *action* as going out there and doing something. They are one and the same. I have done both in my time, and each one has taught me something about this world and how to make my way in it.

As a man, I learned how to handle my pride. That's something that some men never learn. It's a shame too. Pride puts a lot of good men down because it makes them too shortsighted to choose their battles. I figured that one out quick because as crazy as my life was even by the time I was thirteen, I knew this one very important thing: I *loved* life. I didn't come from much and I had even less, but I knew I didn't want to die, I wanted to live. I wanted to make people laugh, I wanted to kiss pretty girls, I wanted all those things that make us more evolved than the animals. I didn't want to kill no one, and I didn't want to lose my chance at trying to make it one more day because I got involved in some bullshit.

I feel like I'm just now putting together all the lessons I've learned. The first lesson that comes to mind when I think of my teens is the differences between men and women. I'm not talking about boys and girls or birds and bees. I already knew all that. In my teens I really learned about men and women—what that bond means, how they need each other, how they treat each other, for better and for worse. And how neither is all that they can be without the help of the other.

Sex aside, a man can't live without a woman. That means different things to different people. Any warm-blooded straight man will do whatever he needs to do to get himself some pussy. But that's not what I'm talking about. I am talking about the *love* of a woman. Not every man experiences that in his lifetime. When a woman *truly* loves a man, he knows it. It's some other shit entirely. Pussy is just one part of it. Pussy and ass and titties are the frosting on that cake. When a woman gives a man her love, it is so much bigger than all that. Thinking about it gets to me because—let me just tell you from the heart—I had that early in life. And I knew it at the time too. A woman possesses the power to transform a man into something better than he would ever be on his own. I don't know how many times women can do that in their life, because it seems like they can only really break it out once or maybe twice. When they do, that shit is magic. They deserve this power, because I don't care what people say—being a woman ain't easy.

But if a woman is the best thing to ever happen to a man, a man can be the worst thing to ever happen to a woman. A man can ruin a woman, and I mean *completely ruin* a woman. I put this together watching my mother after my father left, and nothing in my life since then has proved me wrong. It's the one rule no one can deny: Love might turn a bad woman good, but nothing can turn a good woman back once she's turned bad. That's what happened to my mom, but we'll get to all that.

My first job was packing bags at a Key Food store on Myrtle Avenue right across the street from the Tompkins Houses when I was about eleven years old. Besides the pocket change, one reason I liked to show up was Maria. She was hot. She was the hottest girl ringing up groceries at Key Food, and there was no way I was letting any other motherfucker pack bags at her checkout line on my shift. That wasn't a bad job to have as a kid. If you got a delivery as a bag packer, you got like five bucks just for running some old lady's groceries up to her house, and I wasn't letting any of that money get away from me. I sometimes walked out of there with a hundred dollars on a good day. To a kid, a hundred dollars is a lot of money! I'd use it to buy food at the store or just take it home and give it to my mom, who'd let me keep five dollars for myself. It felt good earning money, and I took that feeling into my adult life. Earning money made me feel like a man, like I was making something of myself in this world.

I've never seen money any other way. I've got friends who want money but don't want to do anything to earn it. They won't hold down a fucking McDonald's job to feed their own kids, but now that I've got money they want to come and work for me. I don't know what the fuck makes them think I want them working for me if they won't get off their ass to provide for their own family. I've lost a lot of friends that way, friends who feel like they deserve a place on my payroll. They don't get it: I don't need an entourage. I don't need to pay motherfuckers to play Xbox with me. I'd rather play Xbox with my kids. Some people get stuck in that mentality. I think it's because they watch too much TV and think what I do must be easy. Don't they know we're in a recession? The only reason my girlfriend won't leave me is because every other motherfucker out there is broke!

Anyway, my teenage years were about three things: football, track, and girls. I learned a lot from pursuing all of them to the fullest. Like a typical stupid teenager, I didn't ask how deep those pools were before I dove in, so a lot of the time I got in over my head. My man Spoon (whom I later immortalized on the Comedy Central show *Crank Yankers*) and I were both stars of the football team, and we used to have hookup parties. We would cut school and get a bottle of Cisco, which is wino shit that's about forty proof and gets you fucked up quick; we'd get some girls, smoke some weed, and then everybody would get on the bed and fuck. We didn't switch girls or nothing like that, but he'd have his girl and I'd have mine and my man Polly would have a girl too, and we'd just all be right there, everybody on the same bed. That was our thing and we'd do it once or twice a week. My brother and I shared a room, my mother had her room, and my little sister and little brother shared a room. We had a hole in the wall too, so when Jim would be in our room with a girl, I could watch him fuck her, and when I was in there with my girl, he could watch me. My poor mother, having three teenage boys at once— we were always sneaking girls up to our rooms. We'd hide them in the closet and under the bed—the typical shit that black males do growing up in urban America.

I had this one girl I'll call K who was a pretty motherfucker; she was tall, with green eyes and long hair. She was younger than me—I was about seventeen and she was fifteen. I made the mistake of taking her out on the streets of Brooklyn, where my dudes were just wolves. They didn't care who your girl was, they'd try to fuck her. I was getting my hair cut by my man Ron, who was older, and she fell for that shit. He had all the things that young girls with no experience fall for: waves in his hair, nice sneakers, a car, and a little cash in his pocket. So he got her. And he gave her crabs! Which that bitch gave right to me. I wasn't with no one else, and I had no idea what crabs or STDs or none of that was. But I found out seven days after we hooked up, when I went to the bathroom and found *things* crawling on me. I could see them on me *everywhere*! My hair down there itched like it was on fire.

I told my mom about it and she started laughing at me. Then she gave me my Medicaid card and sent me to the hospital, where they gave me the shampoo and the little comb. I didn't know what the fuck was going on. But I did know this: Bitches in the ghetto are promiscuous and were not to be trusted. The crab incident didn't help me any with my trust issues as far as females were concerned. The next time I saw K, I chased her down the street with a gun and told her never to show her face in my hood again. That shit scared me so much that to this day I've never had an STD. How stupid would I be if I got one at this point? These days, with all that we know about that shit, how can anyone leave themselves exposed? Everybody and his mom wears condoms now. If you're forty and you show up at the clinic with an explosion of chlamydia, you are one big fucking loser.

Now, by the time I was a teenager, my mother had developed a real frustration with me and a real hatred for my father. She's never said anything to me about it, but I've always thought that since I look just like Jimmy Morgan, she was harder on me than she was on my brothers and sister. She also didn't really give me a lot of attention, which I understand now because my older brother Jimmy's special needs took up so much of her time and energy. But I needed at least a little bit of motherly TLC.

Looking back now I can see that my mother was going through trials and tribulations of her own, trying to raise us while living under the close watch of her strict, religious family. She couldn't deal with me being rebellious. Like every other teenager, I wanted to do things the way I wanted to do them. We fought these little turf wars every day, until she finally threw down the gauntlet. In my second year of junior high school she wouldn't let me play football because she thought I should spend that time studying. I'll never forget the day she shut me down—she would not let me leave the house to go to tryouts. It was fall and I was up in my room looking out the window at all my buddies in the neighborhood leaving their houses with their football gear on, heading to the field. I shouted out the window for one of my friends to wait for me because I was going to go anyway. When I got into the hallway, there was my mother, blocking my path.

"Where you think you're going, Tray?" she asked me.

"To football tryouts. Everyone's going over there now."

"Well, you're not."

"Yes I am! Everyone's going! They're waiting for me downstairs!"

"You're not going, Tray," she said. "You're going straight back to your room right now. That's the *only* place *you're* going." She stood there looking at me hard.

"Why?!"

"Because I said so." And she stared me down until I went back to my room.

I have no idea if she's thought of that moment since then, but that day my heart broke in half. My mom didn't understand that sports were more important to me than anything because they kept me out of trouble. In the hood, being an athlete kept you off the streets, and staying off the streets kept you alive. She did not understand that. I wanted to be Tony Dorsett or Walter Payton. I wanted to chase that dream. I didn't want to get involved with the kind of life I saw all around me.

The next day I went to school with a black cloud over my

head. For a while I had wanted something different for myself. When I'd visit my dad on the weekends, I saw that it was a lot more stable over there. It was fun. My dad would take me fishing. He'd spend time with me and tell me stories. My mother was in many ways a great mother, and she is an amazing woman. But by the time I got to be in my early teens, she had been broken by three men—her father, who was strict and very hard on her; my father, who let her down and broke her heart with his drug addiction; and Sonny, who was a married man. Sonny wasn't the straw that broke the camel's back, but he was the straw that sent the camel to the chiropractor. Back was never the same after that shit. My mother just gave up after that point. That's when she and I started fighting all the time. I was a kid; I wasn't going to understand where she was coming from no more than she could understand my acting out and needing my dad.

It was about that time that my mom turned to gambling. In the ghetto, your local casino is called a numbers hole. My mother started visiting the neighborhood numbers hole, got into gambling, and then she started working there. Once she did that, she'd take my brother, sister, and me down there, which wasn't the best decision, but we didn't care too much; they had Robotron, Ms. Pac-Man, and Donkey Kong games there, and she'd give us quarters all night. I was old enough to know it was wrong, and spending hours there every night well past midnight wasn't fun after too long. I was always afraid of the people that came around there too. I just knew it wasn't a good place to be.

And I was right, because one night when my mother was working and we were there with her, the place got robbed. Luckily nothing violent happened. My mom put us kids in the back room and she handed over whatever money was lying around. But my mother was a stand-up guy; she had the bulk of the money made that night stashed in her bra. She had the money in her titties. Those were good titties too! They fed us, they held the money, they were big—like duffel bags with bowling balls in 'em.

That robbery was a sign of the times: Things were changing at Tompkins; people were starting to get shot. Being with my mother and my brother who was crippled, I never felt protected. It wasn't all that much better up in the Bronx where my dad lived, but I felt like if I were with my dad, I would always be safe. He'd never let anything happen to me, and I hope that's how my sons feel with me.

After a few days of thinking about it, I realized what I had to do. As I passed the train station near our house on my way home from school, I just turned, walked up to the platform, got on the next train out of there, and didn't look back. That decision changed my life *forever*. I've seen ups and I've seen downs since then, and there have been many times when I wished I could turn to my mother for guidance. I've spent a lot of holidays away from her and my brothers and sister, and I've missed them. There have been questions I've wanted to ask her, big questions, but I wasn't able to. And I'm not sure if I'll ever be able to, because when I made my choice that day and got on the train instead of going home to her again, something changed between us that's never been fixed. I went off on my own road and I succeeded on my own terms, and my mother never came along on that ride, because we never patched that up. And we still haven't. I would have loved to have had her come see me at *Saturday Night Live*. She never did. She could have had tickets any week she wanted to for seven years, but she wasn't interested. I know she's got her opinion on it and I've got mine and none of that will change. The day I stepped on that train was the day the space between us opened up; I never lived with my mother again, and to this day we are not close. We're gonna have to work on it.

Whenever I get sad about that, I turn my thoughts to all the good things that came from me taking that step. I might have been pigheaded, but I was right to do what I did. If I had kept on living with my mother, I wouldn't be where I am today, plain and simple. I wouldn't change a thing about how I came up. What I've loved and what I've lost made me who I am. And regardless of how things are, I love my mother and I always will. She did the best she could and I love her for that.

I also love my mother because she got me my first racetrack for Christmas, one of those Tyco tracks with the cars that you put in the little slots. And she was the one who got me my first football uniform when I was about ten years old—the San Diego Chargers. My father never did any of that—it was all my mother. She was the one who went out and got me white football cleats for my birthday because I wanted to be like Joe Namath. I didn't even think I was getting anything that year.

In my heart I do believe that my mom meant well or just didn't realize the effects of her behavior. Since my mother was the one who gave me my first football uniform, the irony of her keeping me from going out for the team was especially hurtful at the time. Looking back on it now, it's all the evidence I need to understand how hard things were for her and how much a stubborn, willful kid like me was for her to take. From the time my father left until he got enough on his feet to help, she'd had to stay on welfare just to get by, raising us all by herself. She stayed in until we were grown up and didn't have to be her charges anymore, and I think that really was tough for her too, because my mother is a proud woman. She's stubborn and strong and that's what has gotten her through this life. When it comes to us, the trouble is that I'm just like her: I may look like my dad and act like my dad, but inside I'm as determined and stubborn as my mama. As a man who survived and strived, I have to say right here that my mother's stubbornness is the greatest gift she ever gave me. If I didn't have that in my DNA, you would not be reading these words at all, because my life would have been over a long time ago.

Back to the afternoon I left home: I got on the A train, and for the next two or three days I slept on the subway at night and went to school during the day. It took two trains to get from where my mom and us kids lived in Brooklyn up to the Bronx where my dad lived: the A train and the D train. I'd get off at 161st Street, Yankee Stadium—that was my dad's stop. I did that loop all night, back and forth from my mom's stop to my dad's stop, for a few days. During the day, I'd be in school and my friends would hook me up with lunch. I spent the few dollars I had to get myself something to eat at night. But I couldn't live like that forever. Damn, I'm just glad nothing happened to me in that short but dangerous period of time. I was tough, but I was still a kid and it was stupid to put myself in that kind of danger. I wasn't a big kid either—if the wrong kid is in that kind of situation even for just a few hours, he might never be heard from again.

I wasn't your average thirteen-year-old because growing up in the hood isn't the same as growing up anywhere else. Kids are wise and too tough for their own good there, you know what I'm saying? There's a reason no kids get abducted in the hood: By the time we're three we know which uncles to stay away from. If you try to snatch a three-year-old in the hood, he'll turn it around on you, steal your car, and call you a fucking pervert. There's a reason why there are no episodes of *To Catch a Predator: Hood Edition*. All those would-be perpetrators would end up as corpses on *Unsolved Mysteries*. I can tell you right now where you can find their bodies. They're buried in a vacant lot. Little Johnny got them with his First Glock.

Riding those trains all night, I knew why I'd rather be cold and hungry than home with my mom: I was out there because I needed to find my dad. I knew where he lived because I saw him every weekend. My mother may have badmouthed him, but she never kept us from seeing him. But spending time with the man is not what I'm talking about. I needed more than that; I needed to find my dad's role in my life. I needed him to be my dad, every day, at least for a while. I'd grown up with male role models, but as puberty was kicking in, my soul cried out for my *dad*. My uncles were one thing, and they were there for me and that was wonderful. But at that point in my life, something switched in my brain and I needed the guidance of the only man in the world I could understand on a deeper level. There is a respect between a father and a son that starts from birth. Now, one or both of them can break that trust, but my dad had never done that with me. He'd done that with my mom, but not with me. And no matter what she said about him, I needed to be near him to learn a different way to live.

After two days of riding the train like a hobo, I showed up on his doorstep in the South Bronx, smelling like ass, just a confused teenage son who'd left his mother's home two hours away in Coney Island with no plan. Jimmy opened the door, shook his head, and didn't ask me any questions until he'd gotten me showered and fed. He already knew what was up: I couldn't be with my mom, I was a hotheaded teenager, and I *needed* him, plain and simple.

There's a sad and funny irony about my father that I only learned when I got to his home. Although he was a touring musician who lived the nightlife and a heroin addict who battled a chemical monster every single day, he had another side that was more responsible than anyone would have guessed. Jimmy Morgan balanced the instability and chaos in his soul with a very grounded, strict home life. He ran his household the way he ran his bands: Everybody had better show up for rehearsal, play his part, and give it his all. It didn't matter to him if the band was playing a dive bar in Mississippi, they had to be as professional as if it was Carnegie Hall. All of the kids in his house had to be the same way.

My dad never got over losing my mother, but about five years after he and my mother separated, he met the woman he eventually married. She let him play his music and make his living that way for the rest of his life—it was his one joy and she understood that. Her name was Gwen. She became my father's rock. Gwen helped him kick the drugs out of his life, but she didn't do it alone. I'm lucky enough to have recently run into one of my father's old friends out of the blue who shed a lot of light on my father's life for me. On July 22, 2009, I did the Letterman show. As I was shopping for the Michael Jackson shirt that I wanted to wear on the show that night, I ran into Vick, who was the bass player in my father's last band. We talked for a while, long and hard, about my dad, and I have to thank him for sharing some details that really made my father's memory come alive. It's one thing to remember your father the way you knew him as a kid, but it's another to speak man-to-man about him with someone who knew him well as an adult.

Vick was a few years younger than my dad, and when they first met, Vick didn't even know that my dad did drugs at all. He could never tell, but slowly it dawned on him. My dad ran with a guy who fronted a local group called Jerry and the Impalas, who were really well known around the neighborhood in their day. Vick went out with them a few times, and that's when Vick realized that Jimmy Morgan and Jerry were into living that late-night musician life and every single thing that came with it—to the fullest. The band Jimmy and Vick had put together was good, and aside from making great music, they were like a family. So the guys in the band told my dad that it was either the drugs or the band, his choice, but he couldn't have both. My dad was in love with Gwen, and she wasn't into any of that either—she'd made it clear to him that he'd lose her too if he didn't kick the habit.

So my father stopped using, plain and simple. He made a choice and he stuck to it. Vick told me how strong my father's character was and how he had such great willpower. Jimmy Morgan never went to a twelve-step program, he just did his own version of it, with the support of Gwen and his friends. Vick also told me that my father and he used to integrate comedy skits into their show. Vick said that singing and writing music were what got my father through the tough times until his mind and body could reject the desire for the drugs on their own. Vick and my dad used to go walking for miles every day to clear his head and get his body back in shape. They'd go, even in the rain, from Nelson Avenue in the Bronx all the way to Central Park and back, which is like seventy or eighty blocks each way! I remember doing that with them one time when I was a teenager and visiting my dad for the weekend. It was incredible, because New York City is the best people-watching city in the world. My father got his inspiration just walking through the hood. That's how he wrote songs. Anyway, meeting Vick was a blessing, because I would have never known these things and I'm grateful to have had the chance. Vick couldn't say enough about my father's fortitude and personality, and it made me happier than he could know.

When my Dad and Gwen got together she already had a baby girl named Yvette, who was about eighteen months old. Jimmy raised her as his own, and the rest of us never considered her anything but our sister. During my teenage years, there were never fewer than two of us kids in my dad's and Gwen's house, but at times there were four, when my little sister, Asia, and my little brother, Paris, joined us, but we will get to that in a moment. They didn't stay as long as I did, but they came for a while, leaving my big brother, Jim, behind with my mom, because he needed extra attention.

Over at my mom's place, I had felt neglected and alone, like I was living in a boardinghouse having to look after myself and my siblings. No one cared what time I came and went. It felt like I was being held back or kept in some kind of neglectful prison. There were upsides, like being able to smoke weed whenever I wanted to. My older brother and I smoked weed there all the time; first we'd try to hide it by spraying shit so my mother wouldn't smell it, but after a while she gave us our privacy and we just smoked it in our room when she was home; she knew what was going on.

My father was a whole other story. He was like a black General Patton. He made sure we were in the house early every night, and since I was playing sports, it was like I'd enrolled in his personal army. He had me lifting weights, running stairs after I'd already practiced with my team for three hours, and when it came to keeping my grades high enough to stay in school, he was even harder on me. In return I got three square meals, including a family dinner every night.

Before I moved in, my father had represented freedom— freedom from my mom, which had to be better than what I had. Yeah, I was free from her, but my dad was reform school. I fought that plenty, but it was the best thing for me. My dad wouldn't let me go wrong; he kept me on the right track. He and I butted heads plenty of times when I first started living with him, but he was my dad. He shaped me, he never deserted me, and he made sure that I came out the best I could be. And even when I was at my worst, being a rebellious teenager, there was no way I was leaving my father. I might never have admitted it to him, but it didn't take me long to see that he was right. I got better at sports and more involved in my school life, and when I'd go back out to Brooklyn, I could see my old friends getting involved in the drug game, deeper and deeper. Before I was even out of junior high school I'd seen enough casualties to count them on two hands.

At first I got into trouble because I fought his rules every step of the way. He was never a pushover; no matter how much damage he'd sustained in the jungle, he was a military man. I think he saw what was going on in my young mind and he knew where I might end up. He took me in to do some good and to be a positive example, regardless of his past. He wasn't going to let that chance to right a wrong slip by him. I'd like to think I offered him a clean slate and a chance at a legacy.

Now that I'm a father myself and have the same responsibilities, I see one thing clearly: My father was teaching us to be self-sufficient. He was preparing us to get the fuck out of his house. He was force-feeding us the skills to survive—to learn the satisfaction of achieving something and earning money, and to learn that hard work, especially for people from our walk of life, was the only way to get by. He took his military approach from his father, who had survived World War II and the Korean War. My father came from a line of men who very early in life had to figure out what tools they needed to survive, and he passed them on to me. Those tools were knowledge, wisdom, blessings, jewels— and my brothers and sisters did not receive them. Even though they lived with our father for a while, they ended up returning to our mother and became dependent on her, more so than I ever was. My brothers and sister still live near her now, all of them out in Ohio together.

I hope this doesn't come off the wrong way, because I really do love my mother and my siblings. We just see life in a different

way. I chose to take my father's road; I chose to work hard and never give up. He was just like that; even when he was on his deathbed, he was still trying to learn something from what he was going through, instead of asking for pity. At the time I didn't appreciate my dad's point of view as much as I should have, but what could I do? I was a teenager, and I was so angry that it took me years to really grasp what he was trying to teach me. Once I was a man and then a parent, I understood better. And that's why I just want to say to my mother once again that I love her and that I'm sorry that we don't get along very well. But I wish her no bad feelings, and I will always love her the only way a son can love his mother—with all his heart.

Anyway, after I got over rebelling against my dad's way of life, I really thrived under his supervision. But soon I started to feel guilty about leaving my siblings behind. I knew I couldn't take Jimmy with me because of his condition, but I could take Asia and Paris. I thought they'd like it better living at Dad's. I used to talk to my dad about the conditions at my mom's house, so he knew what was going on. My brother and sister didn't seem too happy there either. Listen, I was seeing what I wanted to see—I wasn't happy there, so I couldn't believe that they could be happy there either. The truth is, they weren't happy because they didn't have two parents—it didn't matter where they were. They were victims of that tug-of-war that pulls so many kids apart, no matter what kind of family they come from. I'm sure they missed my father; I know my sister did a hell of a lot. My younger brother was a different story because he was only two years old when my parents split up. But all that suffering I saw in them was enough for me because I was suffering too. I thought the only way to erase all of that was to have them join me in Daddy's house, where I was really happy. I did what I thought was the right thing to do and made a plan to get them out of there. It was my version of a prison break; like a teenage Harriet Tubman, I decided that I would smuggle my kinfolk from slavery out in Brooklyn to freedom up in the Bronx. The subway was my Underground Railroad.

One day I went down to Brooklyn and came back with both of them. I showed up at their school and didn't give them a choice: I just said, "Come on, let's go." My little brother, Paris, was crying all the way to the Bronx on the train. He didn't know what the hell was going on.

When we all got back to my dad's, I could see by the look on his face that I'd done some dumb shit. Don't get me wrong, he was happy to see us all, and he knew that he was running a more wholesome household than my mom, but he also knew that me stealing my siblings away like that wasn't going to be all right with my mother in any way, shape, or form. She'd been glad to see her problem child, Tracy, go, but that wasn't a green light for the rest of them to follow me. It was flat-out war between my parents after that, and the start of a custody battle that ended up in family court because my mom went all kinds of crazy. It was a fiasco. My mother kept us enrolled in school out in Brooklyn even though the three of us were living with my dad in the Bronx. For two years, my sister, my brother, and I took the train every day from the Bronx out to Brooklyn to go to school. We were still kids—I was maybe fourteen, my sister was twelve, and my little brother was ten—riding all through the subway system every day because our parents were fighting and couldn't see eye to eye. We were like office workers, getting home at six o'clock because it took that long to commute.

The legal battle escalated. We went to family court because, since we were living with my dad, he was getting welfare checks, and my mother didn't like that one bit. By then she had had another son with her boyfriend, Sonny. Marlon is my youngest brother—he's five years younger than Paris. Anyway, my mother came in with my brother Jim and Marlon and sat on one side of the courtroom, while my father, Asia, Paris, and I sat on the other. It was the first time I'd seen my brothers in a while, and I missed them so much. We were a family torn apart. There were all kinds of accusations thrown back and forth, from my dad's drug use to my mom's gambling habit. I'm glad that I was too young to recall all the details. I can only imagine what they said about each other.

Man, I feel for those judges who preside over family court. They have a difficult job. In a very tough environment, with too many cases and too many people to deal with, they make decisions that will change lives forever. Our judge was this old white man who took me, Paris, and Asia into his chambers, away from my parents, to try to figure out what was best for us. Outside his chambers, the courthouse hallways were noisy, but inside it was real quiet. There were a lot of books and a big table. He sat us down, pulled up a chair, and looked at us for a minute.

"I'm sure you children love both of your parents very much," he said. "But you have to tell me something, and you have to tell me the truth. You can only pick one of them to live with. Who is it going to be? Mom or Dad?"

"I wanna live with my father," I said without hesitation. I looked over at my brother and sister. They were crying.

"I know this is hard for you, kids," the judge said, "but you have to choose." Neither of them said anything for a minute; they just sniffled and tried to talk through it the way little kids do.

"D-d-d-d-daddy," my brother said.

"I, I, I want Daddy, *t-t-t-too,*" my sister said.

"Tracy, both of your parents say that you brought your brother and sister to your father's house. Why did you do that?" the judge asked me.

"I want them to live with me," I said. "I want to live with my dad. It's better over there. I want them with me. I like it there. I think they should be there." By this time my sister had her head down and was crying into her hands and my little brother was crying too and holding my hand.

The judge looked at all of us for what seemed like forever. Then he said, "Thank you, children. Let's go back outside."

He sat down behind the bench and said, "The court rules that custody be granted to Mr. Jimmy Morgan." That was it. Case closed. And that's when my mother screamed like she'd been stabbed. She yelled that they were taking her babies away, and she cried like I'd never seen her do before or since. I'll never forget how much pain she seemed to be in at that moment. She hasn't let me forget that either. I don't think she's forgiven me for it to this day. I know my mom felt like I was the one who let the government take her kids from her, but that wasn't how it was. I didn't want to leave my mother, but I'd found a better life and I needed to share it with my siblings. I think my mother assumed that the judge was going to give her kids back, but the truth was, we really did want to live with my father. We'd settled into the rhythm of life my dad and Gwen provided for us. After that my mom's will to fight for us was really gone.

My mom stayed on welfare until we kids were off her hands, but from that point on she put gambling out of her life. Eventually she got a job as a receptionist and pulled her life together. I had to grow up, get over my youthful anger and frustration, and make a life and a family of my own to realize how much I love and miss my mom. All I hope is that one day we will get together and I will hear her say "I love you." Everything I've done in my career is because I wanted my mother's love. I know she's proud

of me even though we don't speak. I know she's proud. I love her, but what happened happened. I hope she realizes that I'm not mad at her and that, even at my angriest, I always loved her.

Once the custody issue was resolved and I was at my father's house for good, I settled into the best possible home life I could have had. I was definitely damaged goods: My father had to take me to see two psychiatrists during high school because I was so goddamned angry. He just couldn't understand why I was so angry—and neither could I. The truth is, I am still angry, I've just learned to make it work for me. If you take your anger and bend it to your will, it becomes *determination.* And you can get anything done if you're determined. But back then I was years away from seeing that, and so was my dad. He didn't know what to do for me. I was angry at him, I was angry at the world, I was just angry at everybody. Nothing made me happy and nothing made the anger go away.

With a little bit of maturity on my side, I can now see that I was mad at him for not being there all those years. I'd needed him so badly that I couldn't allow the pain to fade away and just enjoy being with my dad. And then once we were finally together, the idea of my dad became reality. He stepped in and took on the authority role, but I wasn't ready for that either. I was angry that he hadn't been there, and then I was angry that he *was* there trying to change my ways. There was no pleasing me, so my teenage years were tough.

Maybe my father felt some invisible clock ticking inside him, counting down the time he had left to teach me what I needed to know, because when I lived with him, even when we were fighting, he would always sit me down and deliver pieces of wisdom.

"Come here, Tray," he'd walk into my room and say.

"What's goin' on, Dad?"

"I need you to listen to me."

"Okay."

"To be a good leader you've got to be a good follower, son."

"Okay."

"You need to follow me. Follow my example and nobody else's."

"I will, Dad," I said. "I will."

And that's what I've done. I'm no fool, and manhood has given me perspective on my dad's faults, but it's also given me perspective on his strengths. I've tried to follow his example on how to be a man, how to handle fatherhood, and how to be a good husband no matter what mistakes I've made. He taught me to respect my responsibilities.

There are so many things that come to mind when I think about my father as a father, now that I am one myself. Most of all, he taught me the importance of being true to your word. He kicked drugs for us; he did what it took. He did what he could to make life special, including taking us fishing. It wasn't *A River Runs Through It,* but my dad got fishing poles, had us all get on our bikes, and led us down under the George Washington Bridge to put some hooks in the water. There was a big hill on the way and my dad was out front and he just started moving down this thing at like forty miles an hour. His fishing bag got caught in his back wheel and the motherfucker flew right off, flipped and landed flat on his back. He just lay there. We all thought he was dead. The skin was all torn off his shoulder, and he really did some damage to the muscles in his arm. But he wasn't going to let that ruin the day. He went to the nearest corner store, got himself some Tylenol, and sat there watching us fish for a few hours be-

fore we all went home. Then he went to the hospital and got
stitched up. That's the kind of man my pops was.

After the custody decision I went to DeWitt Clinton High
School on Mosholu Parkway in the Bronx. I played
football—I was a tailback and my number was 20, after Joe Morris. I love Joe Morris—he played for the Giants and won the
Super Bowl in 1987 with Lawrence Taylor. My son Tracy and I finally got to meet him last year. Anyway, football was already my
sport, but in high school I really came to love track. I played football for my uncle, because he was one of my heroes, but track became my thing because I loved the speed. There is nothing like
running with the wind in your face, giving it all you've got, and
beating everyone running next to you. I was never about distance;
I was always about speed. In my second year of high school I
started running hurdles, both the fifty- and one-hundred-meter,
as well as the fifty-meter dash, the one-hundred-meter dash, and
the two-hundred-meter dash. I was good and really fast. My dad
made sure I stayed that way. He used to make me run stairs every
day in my first year. My next year of track, once I was in good
shape, my dad decided it was time for me to graduate to what he
called the *Exorcist* stairs. A few blocks from our house, they were
three flights up and down. They look just like the stairs in the
movie when the priest is standing there and it's all foggy.

While living with my dad, I fell in love with the Bronx. To
this day I still like driving through there sightseeing and reminiscing. When I was in high school, it was, hands down, the best
time in the history of that place, aside from the early days of jazz.
We lived right next to Yankee Stadium, and it wasn't heaven, but
in summertime it sure felt like it. The lights from the stadium lit

up the entire neighborhood like magic, and all the people who lived there came alive. Those lights set the Boogie Down on fire because a Yankee game meant money. It spelled industry to people who had little else going on but welfare checks. I grew into manhood in the early eighties, right there in the birthplace of hip-hop. The sound that defined a generation was just coming together, and it was happening on my doorstep.

If you wanted to party, all you had to do was head to any park in sight, any night of the week when the weather was warm. You could learn the freshest dances and see all the fly girls, just a block or two from your home. I learned about *life* in the Bronx; it's where I learned how to get my mack on, how to get my comedy on. That's where I learned everything that gave me my flavor.

In high school, traces of the Tracy Morgan that you people out there know today first saw the light of day. That's where I met my man Leroy Elbows and my man Stubbs and all my other homeboys. Not all of them are with us anymore, but I'm still friends with most of them. I'm just one half of this thing I do; those guys are the other side of my funny. Shit, they're just as funny if not more funny than me. I learned how to use comedy in all kinds of situations growing up beside them. We got into and out of so much shit, being on top of our comedy game was a necessity.

From ninth to twelfth grade my friends and I hung out non-stop, and every free minute we had we'd get into these intense snapping sessions. We'd sit there in the hallway at school or in the lunchroom just snapping, sometimes going for like two periods, not even remembering that we were cutting class because we couldn't stop the competition. We'd turn around to see that half our grade had cut class to watch us. If anything, we were like battle rappers—and if you don't know what a battle rapper is, go rent *8 Mile*.

Each of my friends had his own personal comedy style. Mine was to elevate my insult by acting it out. It's hard to explain, but it's like putting an accent on top of an accent and then telling a joke. I never even had to get too nasty with my snaps because my delivery was enough to outclown my opponent. It was another level—not just a funny insult, but a funny insult delivered in an unexpected way. If you don't get what I'm talking about, then you probably don't understand what's funny about my funny at all. It's the same philosophy that informs every sketch and character you've ever seen me do.

In my stand-up I used to contour my body and bend myself around like a crippled person because I grew up with a crippled person. But that wasn't enough to make me laugh, so on top of that I'd act retarded. Then it was funny! People would get all offended, but they didn't understand that I was raised with a crippled person. I know how a crippled person moves better than anybody. Just so everybody knows, my brother Jim loves it when I imitate him. Growing up, I was the only one who could talk about his legs—if anyone else did, both of us were going to fight. Ain't nobody talking about my brother's legs but me. I whupped so much ass because of that.

You might think I was doing wrong in the bigger picture, but you know what? You are incorrect. Making fun of what I see no matter what isn't wrong, it's natural. You should try it! Just keep it to yourselves, because unless you're funny-looking like me and have a God-given comedic gift, you're probably going to get your ass kicked. Unless you're as big as Mike Tyson.

Anyway, in high school, even with all the joking around I did with my friends, sports remained my main focus. We didn't have theater or anything like that in my school, otherwise I'm sure I would have taken my energy there. Sports was the only activity that kept me from getting into trouble full-time on the streets, and like so many kids in the inner city, I thought that I was going to go all the way as a professional athlete. I put all my drive into that instead of school, so by the end of my four years, it was all I really had. I was good—definitely good enough to get a scholarship to college. Who knows where I would be if I'd gone that route?

Something else happened instead: My father was diagnosed with AIDS in my senior year and his rapid decline and death altered my path. I'll never forget the day that I found out. My dad and I had gotten into a fight that morning, and I did one of those stupid things that teenagers do when they're angry: I said some shit I didn't mean. On my way out the door, I was so mad I told him I wished he was dead. I'll always be sorry I said that to him. He didn't deserve that.

When I got home I was still in a bad mood and my dad and I got into it again. It got pretty heated, to the point that I stormed into my room and sat on the bed, staring at the wall with my angry face on. After a few minutes I heard my dad coming down the hall.

"Tray," he said, standing in the doorway.

"What?"

"Guess what?"

"What?"

"You got your wish—I'm dying." He threw down the doctor's report on the bed. "I've got AIDS from doing drugs. And I'm gonna die. So you got your wish."

That was the moment my entire world turned upside down. Everything that was hard in my life meant nothing anymore. I felt sorry for everything that had gone down between us, and I swore to myself that I'd spend every last minute I had with my father. I'd lost him once, and now I was about to lose him for good. I couldn't believe what I'd said to him that morning. I told myself

I'd never fight with him again. I didn't keep that promise either.
For months I was mad at him for dying young.

I had everything going for me at the time: I was a star high school athlete, and I had done well enough to graduate at the end of the year. But knowing my dad was leaving this world made none of it matter. I started skipping school and practice and track meets—all of it. I just wanted to be home with him all day and take care of him as his health started to decline. There was no way of knowing how long my dad had been HIV-positive. He had contracted the virus from dirty needles that he'd used somewhere along the way when he was still shooting heroin. Only God knows how long he had it, because he'd been clean for years, but once it turned the corner and became AIDS, his condition worsened quickly. At that time, in the eighties, the disease was still so unknown; everyone thought you had to be gay to get it and that you could catch it from toilet seats and shaking hands. Today we have drugs that can keep someone with HIV alive for thirty or more years, but back then AIDS was a death sentence, and all doctors could do was watch as a patient was transformed into a skeleton in a few months. It was hard to see my hero lose his strength that way.

One of the last things my dad did before he had to move into the hospital permanently was record two songs that he'd written after he knew he was going to die. He recorded them in our bathroom on his synthesizer. I have those two recordings with me, on my iPod, at all times. One song is called "One by One," which is about him getting right with God, knowing he is going to die. I was sitting there when he recorded it. He was afraid that day and I could see it. He knew it too; we shared that moment together. He was dying of AIDS and he was making it right in the only way he knew how—by writing a song. My dad was so sick that day, he was in his bathrobe, struggling just to make it into the bathroom to record. I offered to bring the keyboard to him in his bed, but he wouldn't have any of that. He loved to record in the bathroom because it had great acoustics. So I helped him get in there, sat him on the toilet, and put the synthesizer across his legs. Then I pushed the buttons for him and let him sit back and play. He was playing and singing to God directly, I could feel that. He wanted to make amends because he knew the time was near.

The other song he recorded is called "Obsession," and it's about my mother. They had that love that I don't think either one of them ever got over. He had found love with my stepmom, but my mother was his first love. You can hear it in the lyrics:

I hear her voice on the telephone
She picks it up but she's not alone
So I hang it up, and I crawl in bed
But I can't sleep 'cause she's in my head.
She's always there
Each night when I go to bed
It just isn't fair. . . . Obsession

Whenever I get sad I listen to the songs because I need to hear my daddy's voice. These two songs are all I have left of the physical memory of him.

I watched my hero go from a strong, strapping man to a withered bag of bones in less than half a year. He got so weak and thin that he couldn't eat solid food, and then soon he couldn't even speak. He'd try to whisper, and all he could eat was pieces of ice. We'd sit there in the hospital and feed him ice while he looked up at us, just helpless, as if he wanted to say something that he couldn't get out. It was heartbreaking.

Once my dad was sick it was hard for me to keep going like nothing was wrong. I tried to keep up a front in school and around most of my friends because how could I share the truth? I was too scared to let it be known that he was dying of AIDS. Ignorance and fear of the disease abounded. If I was honest about it with the kids in school, no one would have talked to me again. I probably would have been expelled by the teachers as a danger to the student body—that's how limited the understanding of the disease was back then. So I kept all of it to myself and let everything that I'd worked so hard to achieve in school slowly slip away from me.

My father died before the end of my senior year. My grades had never been good, but once my dad got sick, they got even worse. The same thing happened with sports—my coaches were great, but my dad was the one who really knew how to motivate me. Once he was gone, there was nobody there to hold me down, nobody to demand to see my report card, nobody to take me down to Yankee Stadium when there was still a track across the street and make me run two miles every night. There was nobody there to watch my football games and nobody to come to my track meets. Nobody to tell me what I was doing right and what I was doing wrong. So I thought, "Fuck it." The world was fucking me. I was on my own.

I started skipping practices and track meets and cutting class. I had been on the track team in 1987 and I had won the Bronx championship in the fifty-yard dash. I was actually going somewhere with that, if I'd only been able to keep my life from ruining my focus. But I couldn't, and I didn't tell any of my coaches why. As my grades started to slip, I began to forge my report cards. I'd carefully change a grade here, make a minus into a plus there, and then I'd turn in that falsified report to my coaches.

They'd put that information onto my transcript, and that's how I kept my grades high enough to keep playing sports. I didn't care at all about school—sports was all I wanted to do. And my coaches turned a blind eye to it. It wasn't a situation that was going to end well, and it didn't. One of the assistant track coaches confronted me just before the team was heading to an important meet. I'd been one of the runners who'd been carrying the team, but that wasn't going to save me.

He told me that I'd been slipping and acting out and that he wasn't standing for it. He said he knew I was forging my grades, and he threatened to go to the school authorities about it. That was it for me; I couldn't take any more. It was hard enough just getting through a school day knowing my dad was one day closer to death. This track coach getting on my case was the end for me: I quit school and never looked back.

Years later I got an honorary diploma from DeWitt Clinton High, which was a surprise to me. I was on *Saturday Night Live* at the time and agreed to appear on a local cable show called *After School,* which showcased a different New York City public high school each week. I was reunited with my track coach, Mr. Brad, my football coach, Mr. Johnson, and my favorite teacher, Mr. Blanco. We shot some footage at the school, and I saw the assistant coach who'd confronted me. He took me down the hall, where there were years of photos of all the sports teams. He stopped at every track team photo for the years I ran track. In all of them, someone, I don't know who, had blacked out my face with a Magic Marker. He was laughing about that; he thought it was really funny, and he made a point of showing me. I don't know what he was expecting, but I turned to him and said, "Don't worry about it, Coach," and walked out of there. Maybe he felt like I let him or the team down back in the day, but I didn't know what to do: I'd been caught forging grades, my dad was dying, and the only thing that made sense to me was to quit school before I got kicked out.

That day I also got to speak to a group of kids in the drama program, which didn't exist when I was in school. It was inspiring to see kids from my neighborhood have that kind of creative outlet. The principal took that moment to inform me that all I'd done in entertainment counted toward four credits in the school's drama program and that I was eligible to graduate. He presented me with a diploma, and I was overwhelmed. Just having that piece of paper and getting to wear that robe for a minute meant the world to me. Right then I knew my dad was looking down on me and was very proud.

After I dropped out of school, I learned a few lessons right away. The most important one was that in high school, pussy is free. That's why they call lunch hour at public school a box lunch. High school was four years of box lunch! I had no idea how good I'd had it in school. It was only after high school, once I found out that just being me, just being funny and flirting with girls I ran into every day, wasn't enough to get me laid anymore, that I realized I had a problem. I hadn't counted on that. I thought that being an athlete made you just as popular on the streets. I was wrong; out in the real world other rules applied. There was one thing that spelled P-U-S-S-Y, and that was M-O-N-E-Y.

I had to find a way to get cash because if I wasn't fly, if I didn't have new sneakers and gear, there wasn't any pussy coming my way. I wanted all that shit because I wanted the girls. Overnight I became a single black male addicted to retail. I needed money, clothes, and hos. There was only one way to get all that: I had to get a real neighborhood job, if you know what I mean. There were plenty of fast-food joints and small businesses, but that's not what I was looking for. I applied where I thought I'd get the most for my time; I started dealing weed. All the kids in the neighborhood thought it was funny.

"You're no drug dealer, Tray, you an athlete! What the fuck you doin'?"

"Naw, man, you want some of this shit?" I'd say. "It's dope, man, best shit on the block!"

I'll be honest: I wasn't the best drug dealer I've ever seen—or you've ever seen either, suburb people! I was the kind of drug dealer who had to keep a day job to support his night job as a drug dealer. You don't hear *that* shit in rap songs. Where's the rapper bragging about slinging McNuggets all day so he can sling weed all night? That was me. I worked everywhere *and* hung out on the block. I needed that nine-to-five. I had jobs at Wendy's, Popeyes, a few pizza shops, and a few sneaker stores, and I was terrible at every single one of them. That's why I had so many! When I worked in restaurants, I dropped all the food. I dropped so many fries on the floor it looked like the Hamburglar ran through there every five minutes. The sneaker place wasn't much better. All I had to do was get shoes from the stockroom in the back, but it's amazing how distracted you can get in a room full of shoes when the stock girl that you like is back there too, telling you about how she just broke up with her man.

The funny thing was, I liked the job I was the worst at—selling drugs. I had my personality going for me; I could talk to people all day, because I love people—I love anyone who wants to give me love back. So as a drug dealer, I was good in only one way—I could talk to any motherfucker that came up to me. But in every other way? Nah. Drug dealers need to be quick, efficient, ruthless, paranoid in a healthy way, and always on guard. I was like half a drug dealer, but that didn't keep me from ending up with all the bad shit that comes with the job, that's for sure.

While I was out there dealing, the drug scene changed right out from under me. Selling weed on the street was nothing once crack came along. Crack. Doesn't it even *sound* like trouble? Crack isn't a natural drug; it's not even a more intense form of a natural drug. It's a concentrated form of a manmade narcotic that dealers cook to save money and increase addiction. Crack was created because a bunch of drug lords in the Bahamas and Miami realized that they had too much cocaine on their hands. They had so much coke that the value of it went down, so they were making less money with every sale. They weren't having that. Since they couldn't increase the demand, they decided to change the drug. They put all that coke into an oven and cooked it up with some other chemicals until it was a pile of high-powered rocks that people smoked. Then they started to market that shit on the streets as the newest high anyone could ever want, at half the price. If there's one thing about Americans, they like the newest shit that does the most. Just turn on late-night TV if you don't believe me. Slap Chop, ShamWow—all that, it's nothing but an eagerness to get there faster.

Once crack became the new black, the South Bronx became New York City's drive-thru restaurant. It was already Easy Street for whatever else you might want, from heroin to coke to weed and hookers. You name it, you could get it in the South Bronx. But crack changed everything. The dude I sold for told all of us soldiers that we had a new game, and I saw the difference right away. This wasn't a party anymore. The people buying crack were serious users. I was selling crack to every kind of person you can imagine: rich people, poor people, young people, old people, desperate people, already high people, and way too many in-withdrawal people. But I didn't care about them too much; I was making money, I was buying myself shit and beginning what I thought was going to be a better life. At the same time I knew it was wrong; it wasn't my character. My grandmother and my uncles and my father hadn't raised a family of jailbirds. We might have had a few drug addicts, but we never had jailbirds, and none of our tribe ever died violently.

I can't lie. There were parts of selling crack that I really liked. Selling drugs to all kinds of people on the street was great for developing my comedy skills. I'd always used humor to get me through tough situations. I took to selling crack like it was an open-mic night, and I was pretty good at it. I had people laughing even when they were jonesing for a fix. Maybe it was just because I had what they were looking for that they were a good audience, but I didn't care. I loved shooting the shit, making jokes with all those crackheads. It was like comedy—they were paying me for a good time.

After maybe a year of standing on the corner making a decent living, I woke up and realized that I was following the herd—and if you follow the herd, you're bound to step in shit. I wasn't stupid; I knew that my new job didn't come with a retirement program. Drug dealers don't need 401(k)s—because they die. I figured that out because my friends started to die. I could name them all here, but out of respect for the dead all I'm going to say is this: A lot of good cats got *washed*. And it was like that all over the country, in every major metropolitan area. I'm sure a lot of you who are about my age understand what I'm about to say: It's one thing to hear about what went down, and it's another thing to have been there, seen it, lived it, and, if you were lucky, to have survived it. I'm talking to those of you like me who might have known what you were doing was dangerous but who were more worried about getting by day to day. It only takes one loss close to your heart to snap your neck around. What you do after that is up to you.

For me, that loss was the death of my friend Spoon. I still miss
him each and every day. We played football together in school.
He was one of the funniest motherfuckers I've ever met. If you
want to know what Spoon was like, get on YouTube and search
for my character Spoonie Luv on Jimmy Kimmel and Adam
Carolla's show *Crank Yankers*. I've got to give it up to those guys
for selling a TV show where puppets act out real live prank
phone calls that comedians like me made. That is *real* right there!
You had be white to make that happen. You think anyone would
have bought that from two black guys? Can you see Redman and
Method Man hosting a show like that? I didn't think so. But who
cares? I'm glad all those executives at Comedy Central are as
ridiculous as they are because that show is a classic, and because it
gave me a place to honor one of my best friends in the whole
world.

At his best, my man Spoon was an insane, dirty, 24–7 prank-
ster. The guy was, hands down, the most on-point wiseass I've
ever met. Spoon always took things that one step further. When
the team used to shower after football practice, we always used to
throw our wet drawers at each other, just fucking around. One
day our coach walked in to talk to us, and Spoonie couldn't help
himself: He threw his drawers at the coach, and they hit him
right in the chest with a loud *bop*! Coach ran us right out of the
showers, he was so pissed, and the next day he made Spoon run
two extra miles in full equipment. Of course, it was those qualities
that also caused his death—that's the way it goes in the ghetto. If
you shine too bright, someone will put your light out. One day
Spoon was out there on the street, doing what he did best—joking
and talking shit to everyone who walked by his piece of pavement.
He started snapping on this one dude and took him *down*. The guy
had nothing to say. Spoon was too good; you had no business get-

ting into it with him unless you knew him and had some ammunition. This guy had none, and he couldn't handle being stripped of his pride.

From what I heard, Spoon wasn't even really breaking his boot off in this guy's ass, he was just being playful, which was actually him at his funniest. But the guy got *pissed.* He had his girl with him, and she was laughing at what Spoon was saying. He was a teenager still caught up in that emotional tornado, a young kid who knew nothing about self-control. Without a word or a warning, he left his girl there on the street, went up into his mama's house right there on the block, got his gun, and put a cap in Spoon's head.

Statistically, Spoon's murder wasn't remarkable—just look at the murder rates in any ghetto in America, whether we're talking about back then or today. There have probably been ten deaths like Spoon's in the time it took you to read the last two pages of this book. Every single day the same type of mindless violence happens in cities across the country. You won't see articles about it regularly in *Newsweek,* but ask anyone in law enforcement. They know because they do the paperwork. There are too many unsolved murders to report on the news. It's too damn common. Spoon was just another one of those.

They say it takes something local to make someone think global, and Spoon's death did that to me. His death was a huge smack in my face. It woke me up and it cut me to my core, because I should have been there with him. I would have been, but I'd gotten lucky that night. I was with a girl who I'd been working on for some time, but if I hadn't been, I'd probably be dead right now. I know this much: If I had been there and that kid came out like that, I'd have taken a bullet because I'd have

been trying to snap on him even harder than Spoon was. I probably would have failed, but that's what Spoon was for me—
inspiration to be funnier because he was so damn quick. It still
makes me pause all these years later when I think about it: If I'd
been there, I'd be dust.

It was like God was looking me in the eye and telling me I was
driving the wrong way down a one-way street. The night I got
the call that Spoon had been killed, I took it as a sign. But there
would be more. My friend Allen got shot too because he followed
a guy named Panama, who was reckless. They were trying to become big-time drug dealers, and I wasn't willing to take it that
far. Remember *Enter the Dragon,* starring Bruce Lee? Remember
the guy he fights at the end, the guy with the claw? He says something to Bruce that I've never forgotten. He says, "There is a
boundary." My boundary was never shaming my family.

I don't know what you believe in, reader, but I believe in *spirits.* I've done some dumb-ass shit, but something has always gotten me through. If you ask me, it's got to be the spirits of my
homeys; they're up there, looking out. They got me, because we
all came from the same beginning. They just got up there first, so
they're watching me now. I feel sorry for the people who don't
have that.

Redd Foxx was the first real dude. He had party albums before Lenny Bruce, and they were so dirty you could not play them around kids. He was a pioneer, straight from vaudeville. He did stand-up for years and then took that spirit and brought it into the sitcom world. *Sanford and Son* was what he did as his third act! And he brought it all mainstream— big-time, mainstream success.

CHAPTER 3

A Home Grows in Harlem

'᾿ve said it before and I'll say it again. I like to say it a few times a day lately, since my girlfriend, Taneisha, and I moved in together: *Nothing* makes a man feel better than a woman. It's nice to have a daily reminder of this in my life once again. I thought those feelings were gone forever after my wife and I split up. We'd been together for twenty years. I thought she was going to be the only true love I'd ever have.

I met Sabina when we were just kids. I was at the age where the last thing you want to do is settle down. At nineteen, every man feels like Christopher Columbus, ready to explore that great ocean of females he sees stretching out to the horizon before him. Nineteen-year-old men are like farmers staring down a field of corn at harvest time, and their dick is the tractor. That tractor is gonna cut into the scrappy, half-bald corn just the way it cuts into those perfect stalks. But that don't matter to a young farmer riding along on his dick tractor. To him, it's all about how many stalks and how quick he mows them down. When you're nineteen and in that frame of mind, *corn is corn.*

I was no different. In fact, it was just that mentality that led me to Sabina in the first place, but once I met her, everything changed. She made me feel like anything was possible. No woman had made me feel that way before. Meeting her, I felt like a kid being introduced to Santa Claus, the Easter Bunny, and a real live unicorn all in the same day. That would be some intense shit!

Sabina was something I didn't think existed—a best friend, a good woman, and my rock all in one. All it took was the love of a good woman to make a man out of me. Within two weeks of meeting her, I was through with other girls and I started to think about building a family of my own.

I'll never forget the day I met Sabina. I was selling souvenirs outside of gate 4 at Yankee Stadium. I had a good business going; I also had my regular coke customers down there too. When it was game time, they knew where to find me—right at my souvenir booth. I'd scalp tickets out there too sometimes. I'd take care of 'em, whatever their needs.

I was standing out there at the stadium on a game night selling shit with my boy Elgis. He is still out there and he is my dog! So when you go to a game at Yankee Stadium and you want to buy some souvenirs, go to the booth right outside of gate 4. You'll see Elgis, doing it like we used to. Tell him Tracy sent you. What up, Elgis! I saw him the other day, the first time I was at the new stadium. That place is nice; it's a palace. Every time I go to a game, it's a trip back in time for me. I see the stairs I used to run, the track I used to jog around, even though they're not there anymore.

So the day I met Sabina I was out there with Elgis, doing our thing. The Yankees were playing the Minnesota Twins, and the Yankees kicked their ass. I remember seeing this bomb-ass chick on a pay phone nearby. She was short with a big fucking booty, wearing these tight cutoff jean shorts. She was looking *good*.

"Elgis, you see Shorty over there?" I asked him. "I could pull her like a hamstring."

"Over there?" he said. "Nah, you can't get her."

"Yes I can."

"Bet."

I went over and stepped to her, and she put up a good fight, but she didn't stand a chance. You've got to understand, I've got the gift of gab—it's the same way I got Taneisha. I made her laugh and I made her smile. No woman can resist me! Give me enough time, and it's a done deal, so long as she's got ears, eyes, and a pussy.

Within a few hours Sabina was on the other side of my booth, helping me sell souvenirs. Next home game, she brought her two kids to the job. Two, maybe three weeks later she finally gave it up and I got some. I took her to this little hotel near the stadium. She was four years older than me and already had two children, but it didn't matter to her at all that I had nothing to my name. I'm glad she saw that I had heart and I wasn't afraid of hard work of any kind. It also helped that I like to be clean. She told me years later that the first night we did it, in that hotel, she was impressed that I'd worn a brand-new outfit and that I washed my drawers out in the sink and laid them out to dry on the radiator so they'd be fresh the next day.

Once the right woman was in my life, that was it. I was happy. I felt a shift in me right away—I was inspired to change. Sabina and I were so right for each other it was like she was my pot and I was her lid, and until you have that, you won't ever understand.

Like I said, when we got together Sabina already had two kids—Malcolm, who was two, and Benji, who was four or five, so there wasn't just the two of us to think about. Her sons were from different fathers, both guys I knew from around the way. That would be a nightmare for most men, but I didn't even care; none of that mattered to my pride. And looking back on it all, I see that the fact that I was cool with the situation says the most about the kind of love Sabina and I shared. Only a real bond with a woman would make a nineteen-year-old male happy to raise two kids who aren't his. Young men in the ghetto are proud and angry; they do not have the ideal temperament to handle raising a neighbor's punk-ass kids. But I saw no shame in it at all; I was proud and happy to raise Sabina's children as my own. To me her children were extensions of *her,* not of those other men. I loved all of her, so how could I not love them? That's how it's been with them from day one. I am their father and they are my kids and that's it. I consider them my flesh and blood. I legally adopted them after we'd been together a few years.

It wasn't long before we added my own flesh and blood to the family. I think my desire began during those three weeks Sabina made me wait before she gave me some of that good stuff. From the first day we met we were together every day, so those three weeks were an eternity. All I could think about was getting some. I wanted it so bad I couldn't even masturbate! I had three weeks of sperm backed up. For the next three years my son Tracy junior was swimming around in my big-ass nuts. When I look at my teenage son now, I like to remind him that once he was just a single sperm cell swimming around in my nuts. Now he's all grown up, got teeth and everything.

Sabina and the kids and I had been together, living in one apartment, for about seven years before she and I even thought to get married! Looking back, I think that's so funny. And at the

same time, I like it. We were too busy just living, being a family,
and enjoying each other. We were already married in our minds.
That's how I thought about it, anyway. For Sabina, who knows?
She's older, and maybe she was waiting to make sure I was good
enough and I was going to stick around. It was a great situation
for me. I got a family and free room and board. But then she
made me earn it. One day I came home from working an afternoon at the stadium and found her ironing the good clothes.

"Baby, what are you doing? Why you ironing the good
clothes? Did somebody die?"

"No," she said. "Nobody died. We're getting married tomor-
row."

"Oh," I said. I thought about it for a minute. "Okay."

She'd already applied for our license, so we went the next
morning to the courthouse in the Bronx and that was it, we were
married. We went down there, and she had her little bouquet.
Our son Tracy junior gave his mother away. Her friend and my
cousin, Lisa, was her bridesmaid. Benji was our ring boy. We
didn't tell nobody; we just went and got married. That's the way
to do it. Marriage ain't about no one else but a man and his wife.

Before I tell you more about my family, I need to take a
minute and tell you about the family member I *almost* had.
This is the kind of fucked-up shit that happens in the ghetto. The
day that my dad died, I came back from the funeral and had to be
alone before I joined my relatives at my grandmother's house. I
was so upset, I just needed some time. As I was sitting there, still
in my suit, looking out the window, I saw this girl walking by. I
called her to come upstairs, and I fucked the shit out of her. Little
did I know that she was fucking everybody else in the neighborhood. I mean *everybody*—she was a real chickenhead, project ho.

A few months later she came to me and said she was pregnant. All my friends, a lot of them who had been fucking her too, tried to give me hints that this wasn't my kid, but I didn't want to hear that. Maybe it was because I had just lost my dad, but all I could think of was that this was my father's first grandchild and I was going to raise it right. This little kid might even be my dad reincarnated.

I had the best intentions as far as the kid went, but that didn't help her and me to get along. I tried anyway. Her family never liked me, which made everything worse. I don't know who they thought they were, but when I came around they acted like a bunch of Nazis and I was the Jew. Even the day the kid was born, they refused to say hello to me at the hospital, acting like I was some stranger in the waiting room. I had the last laugh though, because when the kid was delivered, that baby was *pitch black*. There was no way it was my son; that motherfucker looked *nothing* like me. I nearly doubled over laughing right there in front of her parents. I think I started humming "Billie Jean"—*the kid is not my son, no, no, no.* Kid was darker than the '77 blackout.

She insisted that he was mine, and even though I didn't really believe her, I used to drop off Pampers and bring her milk and food sometimes. This was before I met Sabina; at the time I had a real thug girlfriend who was not having that shit at all. She would go after that bitch when she'd see her on the street, telling her that kid wasn't mine and to stay away from me. I appreciated that. What I did not appreciate was the reaction of my mother and her family—they insisted that the kid *was* mine! I couldn't understand it at all! They'd seen my face since I was a baby. How could they not tell that this kid was some other guy's? That hurt me, man, my own mother not believing me and deciding to treat this girl's son as if he was her grandson.

That was another thing that put a real big wall up between me and my mother. She never really explained why she believed he was my kid—she just did. And once I got involved with my own family and came around less, she'd give me updates on the child, like she was doing me a favor. She had him over all the time for visits. Things got worse when I met Sabina. I thought that would bring my mother and me closer together, because she'd see the good influence Sabina had on me. Sabina got me off the streets, got me away from selling drugs and focused on raising kids and earning money.

But it didn't. She treated Sabina's kids like second-class citizens—even after I legally adopted them. It made no sense to me that she was treating a child who wasn't mine better than the kids I was raising as my own. It got worse when my son Tracy junior came along, because then her preference could not be ignored. She'd make a real big deal over Tracy and never really acknowledged the other two in the same way. And it's not like they couldn't tell—they were definitely old enough to feel that. Any child at any age can feel that. That kind of treatment was something I couldn't agree with, and since she didn't acknowledge the truth in it when I'd bring it up to her, we drifted further apart.

Let me wrap up this story real quick. Fast-forward about eighteen years to 2001, when I appeared in the movie *Little Man* with the Wayans brothers. When I got back from filming in Canada, there was a final notification from the courts about a paternity suit that this girl had brought against me seeking child support. I'd missed the other notifications to reply, so this one said that if I didn't appear at court they were going to give her a de facto judgment in my absence. Good thing shooting wasn't delayed. I went down there with my lawyer and saw that this girl was really bad off. I don't know for sure, but it looked to me like she'd spent the last eighteen years living pretty hard and really needed some money. She had brought this lawsuit, but she couldn't afford a lawyer to represent her, so she was there by herself.

The boy was nice enough. "Hi, Dad! What's going on?" he said. "How's my little brother doing? I want to talk to him. Can we get him on the phone?"

"Let's just wait and see what happens with all of this first, okay?" I said.

It didn't take long to put an end to the charade. My lawyer insisted that we take a paternity test, right then, by order of the court. The judge agreed, and all of us went across the street to where they give the tests. They took blood, did a swab of our cheeks, and the three of us took a picture together. Ten days later we returned to court and got the results. I've kept that piece of paper in my wallet ever since. It said with 99.9 percent accuracy that this kid was not mine. His mother still tried to insist that he was. It was sad. The judge tried to be as kind as he could, but there's no gentle way to tell someone that kind of news. I felt the worst for the kid, though. He was heartbroken. She'd raised him with this illusion for eighteen years, and just like that, you saw it in his face: Everything he'd thought was true about his life was a lie.

Sabina and I weren't afraid to work, and we made ends meet raising our three kids with the help of welfare. But I wanted to make more of myself and felt that I could. I had something inside driving me. Once Tracy junior was born I got myself out of the drug trade because I didn't want to risk leaving my boy without a father. I thought about trying to get a job with UPS or going back to working shifts at a fast-food restaurant or both, but neither idea seemed like the answer. There was always something else nagging at my brain, and I knew I needed to do something about it. For years I'd been snapping on people and entertaining. Right across the street from our apartment there was a chicken shop—it's still there, in fact. Actually nothing much is different in the hood where I grew up because I haven't been out of it that long. I remind people of that all the time. I'm only about fifteen years removed from living in poverty, so I don't know what anybody expects from me. Anyway, the chicken spot was open late, and it had this big open area in the front where I would get upward of thirty people standing around listening to me making fun of shit and talking about everybody that passed by. It seemed to me that doing comedy on a stage couldn't be much different. I started to think about it day and night.

If it worked, it would be my ticket to taking care of the whole family and satisfying this creative urge of mine. This was not the kind of plan most women with three kids living on welfare in a small apartment in the Bronx would want to hear from their husbands.

"Baby," I said to Sabina one night when we were lying in bed. "I can't keep doing what I'm doing forever."

"I know, baby. We'll figure something out."

"I figured it out. I know what I want to do."

"Yeah? You do? What is it?"

"I want to do stand-up comedy."

She was quiet. Real quiet. I turned toward her in the dark, trying to figure out what she was thinking. I was ready for her to yell or smack me in the face, but she didn't do either. She just stayed quiet, looking at the ceiling for a long time—which was worse.

"Listen to me, baby," she finally said. "You are *funny*. You're real funny."

"Yeah?"

"You're funnier than anyone I know. And you're a natural performer, even if there's only one other person in the room. I guess what I'm saying is . . . I think you could do it."

"You *do*?"

"I do," she said. "For real. But if you're going to do it, Tray, you've got to do it *all the way*." She turned over and looked me straight in the eye, dead serious. "You've got to be *focused*. You've got to go for it. You've got to go all the way."

"I will, baby."

"I mean it, Tray. Because this won't just be for you, it will be for *all of us,* so you better mean everything you say."

"I do. I promise."

"I've got you, but you've got to keep at this no matter how hard it gets. You've got to keep at it until you make something of yourself."

Her honesty threw me. I thought about what she said for a long while because I knew how serious she was.

"Sabina, I mean what I'm saying to you. *I want this,*" I said. "And I'll stay at it until I get it."

Thank God it turned out the way it did, because when I told everyone else I was going to be a comedian, they acted like I'd just told the best joke they'd ever heard. Everyone—my relatives, my friends—they all thought it was a crazy idea. And it was, if you think about how few comedians ever see half the career I've had so far.

I had comedy on the mind, but when you have three kids and bills to pay, that don't mean very much. When Tracy junior was born on August 25, 1991, I had already made family my first priority, and I'd stopped selling drugs, because I knew I'd be no good to Sabina or anyone else if I got killed. We were living on welfare up in the Bronx at 1901 Lauren Place. I had my seasonal job at Yankee Stadium and I was trying to bring in money doing stand-up, but I still relied on Section 8 government assistance to get by. Even without a lot of money, living in a room that was smaller than my walk-in closet today, we were happy.

Sabina could have easily turned over one night and said, "Motherfucker, UPS is hiring!" That would have been the last the world heard of Tracy Morgan. But she never said that, and I will always love her for it. She let me *live,* and that's the greatest gift anyone can give to anyone else. If you love someone, set them free.

The other person who really drove me to do stand-up was my man Allen. He had always told me that I was way too funny to be wasting my skills on the corner selling drugs or Yankees jerseys. He was the only other person close to me who believed I could make it, and he knew better than I did at that point—he used to hit all the comedy clubs around the Bronx, probably selling drugs to people up there because drugs is something you can count on finding in a comedy club. Allen told me straight up that I was better than anyone he saw in those clubs, even the ones he'd seen at the Apollo, and as soon as he knew I was seriously thinking about trying it, he damn near dragged me to a club to give it a shot.

Allen was a great friend; he was the first one who came to see my son at the hospital. He's my son's godfather. I was there when Tracy junior was born, right in the room with his mother. I saw him come out of her vagina, I saw them stitch her up, all of that. It was about seven or eight in the morning; then, while they were resting, I went and met my man Al, and he was so happy for me that he cried. He came with me back to the hospital and we saw my son together. "Tray, that is one ugly motherfucker," he said. Then he laughed and hit me off with a thousand dollars.

A month later, to the *day,* Allen was dead, and if it weren't for my son and my family, I would have been dead too. When I was running wild and selling drugs, he and I used to hustle along with this guy Panama and this guy Sweets. That was my crew, but the difference between me and them is that I was selling drugs just to get a little extra roller-rink money and some new sneakers; the other dudes wanted to be big-time dealers. Panama was one of those dudes you just knew was dangerous. He wanted to make an empire for himself, even if it was just a few corners. And he was a hothead too.

It's a typical story. Allen and Panama were having a territory issue with another drug dealer up in the projects who had workers dealing right across the street from them. I guess there was too much crack and not enough crackheads, so Panama kept beating up the guy's workers to drive them away from their corner. We knew the guy too—all of us went to junior high school together. It just goes to show you, 99 percent of murder victims are murdered by people they know. Anyway, Panama used to beat the guy's workers up, and Allen used to go over there with him. I told Al that he had to stop following Panama because he was trouble, I could just tell. Panama had the big jewelry and the nice car, all of which impressed Allen. Anyway, when the guy put his kids on the corner again, Allen and Panama went over to talk to him about it. The guy saw them coming, must have gotten scared, and came out of the building with a .357 and started blasting both of them. Allen died that day. Panama held on for about two weeks in the ICU and then died. We were all around twenty at the time.

Allen's death was that last push I needed to step into a comedy club and go for it. I thought that even if I did terribly, I had to at least try, to honor his memory. Part of my problem was that even though Allen and Sabina, the two people closest to me, believed that I could make it, I'd learned never to believe anything people told me about myself. My dad had impressed that on me early in

life, back when I was an athlete and coaches and everyone were
forcing their expectations on me.

"Tracy," he said to me at that very crucial time, "don't believe the hype. Do not listen to anyone but *yourself*. Everyone is going to tell you you're great until you're not great. Until the day you let them down. And on that day they'll hate you. If you listen to what other people think of you, you'll need them. How you do and how you think you do will matter less to you than what other people think."

"So what, Dad?" I said. "So what if people say things about me and I care about it?"

"So what? What do you mean *so what?*" he said. "Listen to me, son, and don't you forget this: A man can't need anyone but himself in this world. If a man needs anybody else, *he's a dead man*."

I just stared at him.

"It's the truth, son. And don't you ever forget it."

He had been talking about my athletic career at the time, but I've never forgotten his advice. Nothing that's happened to me in my life since then has ever proved him wrong. It's one of the lessons I carry with me every day. I think it's kept me in check, except for those few years when my train went off the tracks.

Doing stand-up, I learned right away that you've got to be willing to dig a hole for yourself, then build your way out of it right there onstage, each and every time you perform. People think digging a hole is trapping yourself. It doesn't have to be— it can also be how you let yourself grow. It can be how you win over the audience too. Look at it this way: If you want a tree, you start by digging a hole. Then you plant your seeds, you water them, and you wait for rain and sunshine to do their thing. After a while, if you take good care of it, you've got a tree. That's how I let a lot of my stand-up sets develop. And in the bigger picture, that's how I see myself today—I am still that tree. I started from a seed in a hole and now I'm out of the ground, still growing strong out into the world and up toward the sky. I look back on the days when I decided to pursue comedy as the moment I dug my hole. I dug a lot of them, in every hole-in-the-wall club I could find, and I planted seeds in every single one of them too.

Once I got over my fear, it didn't matter to me if I bombed onstage because no matter what happened, when I came home, I was *good*. I was a daddy, I was a husband, and I was never pressured to do anything but try my hardest to pursue my dream. My lady was never behind me because she knew I didn't like to be pushed. She was never in front of me because she knew I didn't like to be pulled. She was where she belonged—right by my side. I was never gonna lose as long as I had that support. When I had a bad set, she'd just say, "Go get 'em next time."

It's amazing to me how much Sabina and I shared with each other, even though we were so young. I loved to lie in bed with her after the kids were asleep and talk about life. In those moments of pillow talk, Sabina taught me all about women's minds and how to relate to the opposite sex just by telling me what she was thinking and how she was feeling. She didn't even know how much she was helping my career by solving those mysteries for me, but all of her insight definitely contributed to my success. The guys with degrees in marketing from expensive private colleges tell me that the group that reacts to me the strongest on *30 Rock* is women. That's when you know you've made it—when the women are your biggest audience. If you've got the women in your corner, you're Will Smith, Denzel, or LL Cool J. If you've just got the dudes, you're Wesley Snipes or Iron Mike Tyson.

I think I owe my female fan base to my ex-wife. Nights when I could have been hanging out with the boys, she gave me a reason to want to be home, expanding my view of the world by opening myself up to her. Baring my soul like that didn't come easy. Growing up the way I did, I was more inclined to keep my true self locked up inside and well protected. But Sabina changed all that; she showed me that keeping your sensitive side alive and well is important. It's what sets you apart, especially if your focus is comedy. When I started to perform and to act, she reminded me to show that part of myself. That's why I'm glad I got to cry in my movie *First Sunday*—women *love* to see a grown man cry because that shit is *moving.* Am I right? You ladies on *The View* hear me? The only way you can top crying in a major feature film is by crying on Oprah. That is the be-all and end-all. That's the Oscars of crying! In terms of sensitivity, you've arrived if you cry on Oprah. When you're on that couch crying, it's like having your soul do a striptease for the world. That is allowing yourself to be truly vulnerable, and being vulnerable is nothing but a sign of real strength.

Sabina knew that back then because she's a very wise woman. I missed her for a long time when we split up in 2007. As you're going to see in the next few chapters, we really had a ride together, with lots of ups and downs. It was strange for me to learn to live without her. It was like losing an arm: I survived but I had to learn to drive different. It looked like we were going to get back together for a while, and it looked like we were cool, but divorces are never easy. We're not cool anymore, but I still have to thank her for having class about our breakup. When reporters came to her house after the news of our divorce broke, she didn't go off on me. She pretended she was the housekeeper and said, "I'm sorry, Mrs. Morgan's not home."

I can still say this from the bottom of my heart: I'd do anything for Sabina. She was never possessive with me, she was always my best friend and my first true love, and she'll always have a piece of my heart. But people change, and that's what happened to us. You'll see what I mean shortly.

Comedy in the late seventies and eighties was just becoming the big business it is today. Places like Caroline's in New York, the Comedy Connection in Boston, and the Comedy Store in L.A. were places where comics could make a name for themselves. They had nice stage lights and carpeting and mixed drinks that weren't watered down. I wasn't playing gigs anywhere like that when I started. I did stand-up at every open-mic night in the Bronx and any comedy club that would give me five minutes of time.

There was a comedy scene up in the Bronx, in a bunch of clubs that usually smelled like old beer or stank ass. There were a lot of talented comedians, but many of them didn't make it. There were people like Faceman, who was hilarious but became a serious drug addict; there was Uncle Jimmy Mack, Brooklyn Mike, A. G. White, and Doo Doo Brown, who was great; Jim Breuer and Ronda Fowler, who've done things here and there. No matter who was on the bill, you could be sure that the club was going to be packed with rowdy motherfuckers from around the neighborhood who wouldn't keep their mouths shut. Being onstage in a black club is like trying to do comedy in the street—there's no division between the show and the audience, and if the comedian isn't good, you'll at least be entertained by the crowd. When you do comedy in front of a white audience and you're not good, they just sit there. They don't always boo; usually they just don't say anything. Black audiences ain't like that. They let you know right away. They boo real loud and usually they throw stuff.

Doing comedy in those small clubs was a test of survival. You have to bring it, because black people like to see people fail like a motherfucker up there. They get into booing you off all together, like fans doing the wave at a football game.

That doesn't happen to me now that I'm established. These days I usually come on to a standing ovation, which I never get tired of, but I've seen my share of booings. The worst for me was probably the second time I played the legendary Apollo Theater in 1992, after I'd been doing comedy for a few years. The first time I played the Apollo, I got up and did a short set and I killed. I had them rolling, got the standing O, all of that. So my manager got me booked there a few weeks later. I made a very serious mistake that time—I let all of the love I got the first time go to my head. I let my ego interfere and thought that since they loved me so much, I'd be fine going out there and trying out new material that I'd never tested before a live audience.

I had a seven-minute set. Seven minutes doesn't sound like a long time. That's about two rap songs or two movie trailers. Seven minutes is about half the amount of commercials you're going to watch during your typical one-hour TV show. It may not seem like a lot, but when you're onstage bombing, it feels like a year. I went out there, and from the first joke I was bombing. I got about two minutes into my routine when I heard this big lady up in the balcony start booing as hard as she could. It spread like a case of herpes, and soon the whole place was yelling for me to get pulled offstage.

For those of you who don't know, since the 1950s the Apollo has employed the Executioner, played by Sandman Sims, a famous tap dancer from back in the old days who'd been dancing at the Apollo since the forties. The Executioner would be at the side of the stage, in the wings, and when an entertainer got booed, he'd come out and chase him off with a toy gun or pull him off with a giant hook. So I'm bombing and I look over and see Sandman stretching, getting ready to come get me. He's picking up his hook and eyeing me and starts to walk onstage. I wasn't going to let him pull me off, so I looked at him and said, "Fuck you!" Then I looked at the audience and said, "And fuck you!" and I ran off.

There is another custom for amateur talent at the Apollo, this one a good-luck tradition. Positioned to the side of the stage is the Lucky Log, a piece of what was known as Harlem's "Tree of Hope," a large elm that supposedly brought good luck to all who touched it back during the Harlem Renaissance in the twenties and thirties. When the streets of Harlem were widened, the elm was taken down and chunks of it were sold off as souvenirs. The Apollo got a big piece, named it the Lucky Log, and placed it where every amateur performer could touch it before going onstage. Well, I knocked that motherfucker right over on my way out. I just knocked it right into the audience. And because of that I was banned from the Apollo for two years.

I got off to a much better start at the Uptown Comedy Club on 133rd Street, not far from the Apollo. That's where everything came together for me.

My boy Mike Greg, who was a friend from around the way, told me about it. He said the place had a weekly open-mic night and a Wednesday-night workshop to help out aspiring comedians. He thought I could get up there and hold my own with anyone he'd seen come through, no problem.

I went to the club with him one Friday night. I was a little bit apprehensive, but I wanted to see what it was all about. There was a twenty-dollar cover charge, which I wasn't willing to pay, so I watched from the door for a minute before the bouncer moved me along. But it was enough time to see one really good

comedian, and that was motivation enough for me to go back on
Wednesday for the workshop. That place really taught me how
to do my job. It was run by Andre Brown, who taught everyone
who came through the door the fundamentals. It was the comedy
equivalent of playing Little League baseball. I learned how to
hold the microphone properly, how to use my environment onstage, how to hit pockets of different energy. I also learned how to
segue and how to bring the mood from one subject to another
and let the crowd's energy ebb and flow. I liked having someone
show me how to take what I was doing more seriously and how
to approach it as a craft. I had never even been in a school play or
taken a drama course or anything, so this was the first time I was
made to think about the fundamentals of performance.

The most important knowledge I took away from there was
about commanding the crowd. I still think of a few basic tips
when I get nervous about taking the stage. Yes, I still get nervous.
I think any good performer, no matter how good, gets nervous.
It's healthy to treat every performance like it's your last. Anyway, what I try to remember is to show confidence, to move
around, and to stay loose physically. If you tighten up, you look
scared, and if you look scared you will lose command of the audience. The second-most important thing to remember is to have
fun up there. If you're not having fun, the audience isn't going to
have fun. Even if they boo you, you've succeeded, because if they
have fun doing that—fine! At least they got their money's worth.
You just have to enjoy whatever happens and be ready for it.

I started rocking things at the workshop. Within two weeks I
was getting regular spots at the club, and I was killing it there too.
There was a real hot scene going on in that place at the time, and
a network guy from Fox TV decided to develop the talent he saw
into a weekly sketch-comedy show that would be like *Live from*

the Apollo but all comedy. It aired for two years, from 1992 to 1994, and it was responsible for the launch of a few careers, namely, mine and Chris Tucker's.

I have to take a minute to thank the entire Brown family: Andre, Kevin, and their mother, Mrs. Brown. Andre taught me the basic skills I needed to handle myself on a stage. His brother Kevin gave me my first break on television, and shortly thereafter he and Andre became my managers. And most of all Mrs. Brown, who was always reassuring and who signed me up to do my first appearance at the club. Kevin Brown, by the way, plays Dot Com on *30 Rock,* so I still work with him. It's great to have that connection.

Uptown Comedy Club aired at the same time as *Saturday Night Live,* which was fine because we were built for a much different audience. Now that I'm more familiar with the language of marketing demographics, I'd label our target audience as nonwhites who own televisions. We did sketches meant for people living in urban America, dealing with all that comes with that. One week, Chris Tucker was supposed to headline the show but his plane from L.A. was late and he wasn't going to make it for the broadcast. I had done a few sketches and was still doing bits in the regular club all week long, so Kevin came backstage and found me.

"Yo, Tray, what's up?"

"What's up, Kev? What's goin' on?"

"I hear you're fire in the club. You're a fan favorite."

"Yeah, I guess so."

"So you got seven minutes? You want to go on?"

"I got seven minutes for you."

And I never looked back.

I was kinda fat back then, which never hurts nobody in comedy, so I used it to my advantage in my act. Fuck sexy, I brought chubby back. It made me even cuter onstage than I already was.

If you're fat, you suffer from inflated food bills, bad knees, broken furniture, and heart problems. But in comedy, you're way
funnier. I used my extra weight to transform myself into a pouty
little kid.

Today my stand-up material is based on observation, but back
then I made up bits based on my imagination, my daydreams,
and that night I did one that I'd been working on for some time:
fat Michael Jackson. I got up onstage and told the audience I was
Michael's fifth cousin, the one who'd taught him how to dance
and everything else he knew. I pulled out a dirty white sock with
a hole in it and wore it on one hand, tucked in my shirt to show
off my fat ass, and pulled the white socks on my feet all the way
up to my knees. I started dancing and spinning around, then I
opened up my shirt and slapped my stomach, grabbed my dick,
and pointed my toe. I did all that "Hee-hee!" stuff Michael does,
and they loved it.

I also brought out my favorite character from the time, one
who is still dear to my heart. He's a little boy from the ghetto
named Biscuit. Biscuit wears one of those beanie hats with a propeller on it and some shorts, and he's angry at everybody because
his daddy left the family. He became real popular on *Uptown
Comedy Club,* so I brought him back a few times. My favorite bit
was when Biscuit got so mad about his dad leaving his mom that
he beat up Barney. I think people enjoyed seeing that on national
television. I knew plenty of parents who were ready to peel Barney's cap themselves after overexposure to that "I Love You"
song.

That was my big break. It was the start of Kevin being able to
book me gigs outside of New York City, and I took every single
one he could get. The only problem was, he wasn't getting me
enough. I was hungry, I had a family to feed, and once I felt what
it was like to do my thing onstage, I was insatiable. I wanted the

next room and the next challenge. I had to push Kevin to get me bookings outside of the Uptown, and even I knew that if a manager believes in his client, the client shouldn't be convincing him to find work. Sabina and I always thought that Kevin wasn't pushing me as much as he was his other clients, and Sabina called a few clubs outside the New York area that Kevin said had turned me down, and they'd never heard of me. Kevin never admitted to that, and we never confronted him about it. It didn't matter anyway—he just wasn't doing his job. I remember when it all came to a head. Sabina and I were at Meineke getting the muffler on our car fixed. Times were tough, we had bills, and Kevin wasn't getting me work. Sabina had had enough and she called him up.

"Kevin," she said. "Listen, Tracy has a family and we have bills and he needs to get some work. He will go on anywhere, he's ready to work. Just book him in and tell him where to go. We need the money."

"I'm doing everything I can," he said. "You'll be fine. Are you guys on welfare?"

Sabina was taken aback a bit. "Uh," she said. "Yeah, we are."

"Well, stay on it," Kevin said. "We'll get him work, but stay on welfare. They owe you that."

I didn't talk to Kev for a while after that, but eventually we came back together and reconciled. In fact, we work together these days—he plays Dot Com on *30 Rock*. We're all family.

In high school, I was one of those people voted most unlikely— most unlikely to do anything with his life or to be remembered by anybody except his family. People like me were thought of as red slimy slugs crawling around on our stomachs in the dirt. We weren't slugs, we were just caterpillars waiting to transform. The people around us were animals, soaring and running, while we just crawled by, waiting for our time. Sure, some of us got stepped on by mean people or eaten by birds along the way, but those of us who survived found our branches, went quietly into our cocoons, and went to *work*. And now all of us are beautiful butterflies. We've had our day.

You know what I love the most about being a beautiful butterfly? Seeing the people who knew me when I was a caterpillar. They're so quick to tell me, "I knew it, Tray! Back then I knew it. I knew you'd be a beautiful butterfly!" Fuck you, no you didn't. You can't predict the future. If you could, you probably would have been more supportive of all the caterpillars you knew. We could have used your support then, but we sure don't need it now. But that's all right with me. The truth is, no one sees transformation like that coming—not even the caterpillar.

BLACK COMEDY IS
Richard Pryor

The two sweetest words in comedy: Richard Pryor. The comic's comic. He exposed everything about himself—from the pain of growing up in a whorehouse to revealing his issues with sex and drugs—and didn't care who liked it. It took a big man to talk about getting high and getting thrown out of his house. He lit himself on fire and went right back onstage after that! He's like Slick Rick—Richard lived out his stories like Rick lived out his lyrics. Richard lived it hard and told us all about it afterward. He went on national TV, looked at Barbara Walters, and said, "I was doing some cocaine. . . ." That took a lot in those days, man. It's the blueprint right there.

CHAPTER 4

Ready for Prime Time?

set foot on an airplane for the first time in 1993. I was twenty-five years old. By then I had become a regular on *Uptown Comedy Club,* and because the show had a solid reputation on the comedy circuit, I was able to expand my fan base beyond the New York metropolitan area. It was incredible to show up at a club in Boston or Philly and find audiences who actually knew who I was.

When *Uptown Comedy Club* went on hiatus, my manager booked as many shows as possible for me, and that's how I ended up on a plane to St. Louis. To me, even a short plane flight like that was like going to Disneyland. I hadn't been there either, but I had heard good things about it. The closest I'd been to a plane was seeing them fly over my neighborhood every day. Vacationing wasn't something people did much in the hood. When they did, it usually involved going somewhere by car or bus, some-place close like Coney Island or just fishing in the Hudson River down under one of the bridges. I had no idea how an airport worked. When I went through security and they asked to see my ID, I put my hands behind my back because I thought I was being arrested. When someone with a badge asks you to empty your pockets, usually you're up against a wall, so I didn't know what was going on. Now I fly all the time and I've gotten used to it, but that first time, when the engines started up and we rolled down the runway, it felt to me like the most unnatural thing in the world.

The gig in St. Louis was in a club called the Bank, which was in a renovated bank, right in the middle of downtown. To a kid from Brooklyn, it was surreal. It really was one of those moments in my life where I felt like I'd done something big. I remember calling Sabina from the hotel room and sharing a "we did it" mo-ment. It was an amazing first-time experience on the road—the gig was great, I killed, and I came home feeling like the king of the world.

Traveling out of town didn't always give me that same high, however. I did one gig in Montreal that was probably the worst bomb I ever dropped. My manager had gotten me on the bill at a comedy festival up there, and I was ready to bring it. I arrived and found out that most of the audience was from Montreal and spoke French. A lot of the comics on the bill did their act in French. And there I was, some motherfucker from the projects, going out there onstage doing my little project jokes. I'm up there in the spotlight wearing my beanie with the propeller on it, doing my thing, and it was as quiet as a morgue. I'm listening for any kind of reaction, and hearing *nothing*. I mean, nothing at all: no booing, no little comments here and there, no talking whatsoever.

That's not true, actually; I heard a waitress all the way over at the bar whisper to the bartender that she needed three rum and cokes. I stayed loose and tried to have fun up there, but this was bad. I could hear someone smoking in the back of the room; with every drag I heard the crackle of the cigarette burning down. I'd never been in a room that was so silent. I felt like I was doing my act in a closet with no air.

When I got offstage I was distraught. I had gone up there expecting to take down the whole festival and make a name for myself! A lot of comedians, agents, and film executives were in the audience—just the people I wanted to impress. By the time I got offstage I was crying, just standing there backstage, ashamed and embarrassed, not knowing what to do. Tommy Davidson, who is a great comedian, came up to me and tried to make me feel better.

"I deserved it," I said, trying to stop crying.

"Listen to me, Tracy," he said. "If you're going to become a good surgeon, you're going to lose a few patients. Let it go. You cannot let one show make you or break you."

I've never forgotten that, but at the time it didn't help me. I went to my hotel room and refused to come out for the remaining three days of the festival. It was the first lesson I got in adapting. I had to learn to adapt for every audience I saw. I wasn't just going to be in front of purely urban audiences anymore. I had to learn to keep my style intact but to expand my repertoire. I've learned that a true comedian never forgets who he is and he always remembers *where* he is.

If you want to make something of yourself in this world, you have to work hard for it. Just going through the motions isn't enough. If it was as easy as an exercise program, anyone could be successful. To make it, you have to put all of your mental energy into achieving your goal, and you need to do it for much longer than you probably think. You need to do it until you don't think you can anymore. You need to keep going, past the point of giving up. And then you need to push yourself some more.

After a while, you'll start to see that effort pay off. It may not even happen to you the way you intended at the start, but if you've really given it your heart, your efforts will be rewarded. It'll be like a snowball of greatness, rolling downhill, that will take you with it. That same rule applies to negative energy. If you're a hater and you focus your energy on anger and negativity, all of it will come back at you. I don't think most haters realize that. They think getting hate off their chests means it's gone because they've put it on some other person. They might be rid of it for the moment, but it doesn't disappear. It's out there getting stronger, getting ready to return to its master, bigger and badder than before. Life is simple if you follow one rule of thumb, people: You get what you give. You don't have to believe me, but as far as I'm concerned, it's the truth.

Long before all my bad stuff came back to me, my snowball of greatness came rolling down the hill. And not exactly how I expected it to, either. In 1993 I got booked for an appearance on HBO's *Def Comedy Jam,* which was the top live-television venue for comedians like myself. That night was even more special because it was my wife's birthday. There was no greater gift I could have given her, because my success was hers too. Sabina wasn't the kind of woman who would be backstage saying, "Baby, you're going to be fine, don't worry." Here's what she said: "Motherfucker, you better get out there and tear that shit *down.* Fuck all these other comedians. Tear that shit DOWN!" She meant it too.

Like I said, the payoff for your hard work doesn't always announce itself. I was happy enough just to make it onto *Def Comedy Jam,* but that night held more opportunities for me than I knew because that was the night I met Martin Lawrence. From my dressing room, I heard a friend who was writing for Martin coming down the stairs, so I went out to say hello, and there on the stairs was Martin himself. He wasn't my idol, but he was an inspiration to me. Martin was someone who made me think my dreams were possible.

Martin introduced me onstage, and when he handed me the mic, I patted him on the ass and said, "That was a good pass, man. Good pass." He watched me do my set and just fell in love with me. "You remind me of me," he said to me backstage. "We have to do something together."

It didn't happen right away, but when it did, everything changed as quick as if someone flipped a lightswitch. After the *Uptown Comedy Club* got canceled, I kept doing my thing, playing gigs and traveling when the opportunities were there. Then one morning I got a phone call. I was outside at the time, putting my sons on the school bus. When I got back upstairs, Sabina told me that Martin Lawrence had called and that he was going to call back in ten minutes.

"What?" I hollered. "What'd he say?"

"He wants you to come do his show!"

"You're lying, motherfucker!"

"No, I'm not! He's gonna call back any minute!"

Then the phone rang.

"Hello?" I said.

"Tracy."

"What up?"

"It's Martin."

"Martin! What's happenin', chief?" I said.

"Nothin', man," he said. "Tray, we got a character for you on my show. I want you to come out to L.A. this week. Can you do that?"

"Yeah, I can swing it."

By seven o'clock that evening I was on a plane to L.A. for the first time. We shot my first episode as Hustle Man on *Martin* the next day. It was the episode where I sold him some ties. I was so intimidated going into the studio! This was Martin Lawrence's show! It was one of the most popular sitcoms on television at the time. What the hell was I going to bring to that?

From the first time I met him, I've always been able to make Martin laugh. Nothing's changed either: I recently shot the film *Death at a Funeral* with Martin and Chris Rock and had them laughing on set the whole time. Martin told me that he had wanted to come up with a character for me on his show, and Hustle Man was it. I can see why too; back then I was hustling my act, always looking for ways to get somewhere better in show business. I was hungry, like that dealer on the corner, like that hustler. In my comedy, I was taking what I found on the streets of the ghetto and selling it to anyone I could, promising them that it was just the thing they were looking for. There wasn't a comedic actor around that could play Hustle Man better than me, because it wasn't much of a stretch. Besides, that catchphrase "What's happenin', chief?"—I'd been saying that for years.

I was nervous on the set, so I did the only thing I could think of to calm down: I drank a little gin and juice, just like Snoop said to. It made sense to me at the time, and being loosened up like that didn't hurt my performance any, I can tell you that. Or maybe it did, but I was too young and dumb to know the difference. Unfortunately, using alcohol to calm myself ended up becoming something—a habit and a problem. I used a crutch to get me through that first door, and it became a tradition. I thought the only way to walk on was to keep using that crutch, because that's how I started.

I had butterflies in my stomach on the set that day. Those butterflies are your nerves going crazy, reminding you that what you're about to do is important, so you'd better bring your best. People who go onstage for a living learn to use them, and a lot of people say they look forward to that feeling. It's the fire that gets them going. Not me—nerves is nerves. Those butterflies are there to make sure I do my best by making me think about when I've done my worst. They don't fuel my fire; they keep me humble. It's been over ten years since that first day on the set of *Martin,* but the butterflies are still with me. I've seen many stages and many sets since then, but no matter what the size of the venue, no matter whether I'm performing live or on tape, those little bugs flying circles inside my stomach keep me *real.* We've learned to work together; once I'm in the motion of a performance, they go back into their cage. But the truth is, they don't stop fluttering until the camera stops rolling or the curtain goes down. Then their cousins, the worry bugs, take over—they're the ones that make me worry about my next move up the ladder.

Martin was my first time on a real network-TV show, with multi-camera production and lighting, a big-time production crew, and a live studio audience. I'm glad I jumped right into the real thing! Martin was the guy who let me live—he brought me on his show and allowed me to do my thing. He let me improvise because he trusted me. There was a lot of stuff I did that didn't make the show, I can tell you that much. My goal was always to make Martin laugh—because it was his show! Besides, if you're a comedian and you're getting laughs out of someone you look up to, there is no better feeling. Martin Lawrence to me was like the moon barking at the dog. The saying is that it's common for dogs to bark at the moon, but if the moon barks at a dog, that dog is famous. Martin is one of the funniest people on the planet, and at the time he had the hottest and funniest sitcom on the air. Once people saw me making *him* laugh, they were like, "Oh, shit, this guy Tracy Morgan, he's gotta be famous!"

Hustle Man appeared in six episodes of *Martin* over two of the five years the show was on the air. The audiences liked him. During my time on the show, Martin and I got real tight. I'd hang at his crib when I was in L.A. to shoot, and whenever he came to New York we'd hook up. When Martin was in town, I'd be the one to pick him up a couple of ravioli bags, if you know what I mean (I'm talking about weed), and then we'd head out and hit the clubs. We did it like that, just real life.

We hung out a lot. That was the great thing about Martin: Considering where he was in his career and how much he had achieved, he never talked down to me or lectured like he knew it all, he just gave me knowledge that could help me in my career. Martin never talked to me about the funny; he never tampered with that. That was a gift God gave me. What Martin did teach me about was the business of show business. He told me about a few battles he'd had to fight to get where he was, and how he learned to pick and choose them as he got more experienced. He really taught me that it was important not to turn every fight into a battle, whether you were working on a TV show or doing a stand-up gig for a promoter who didn't do right by you. Martin was always gracious, which I also saw on his set. He treated the guys who worked for him with respect, and he always had fun with the audiences at his show. He was never above anybody in his mind; he and his audience were the same. It was a blessing for me to be exposed to an artist of his caliber when I was just starting out, because he showed me how to handle myself.

At the time, Martin was going through his own trials and tribulations. He'd had some legal issues surrounding his show that nearly caused it to be canceled before the final season. He'd gotten into drugs a little too much, and they'd brought on some erratic behavior on a movie set. Then he got arrested for going a little crazy with a pistol out on Ventura Boulevard. I listened to him talk about his troubles, but I really couldn't understand what he was going through. I wasn't rich and I wasn't famous. I knew about pressure and stress, but not at his level. I was still just about surviving, which comes with a whole other kind of pressure and stress.

Success and celebrity bring you a lot of money and a lot of good, but they also bring bullshit and expectations, and everyone reacts to that differently. When you come from nothing, sometimes you're your own worst enemy. But no matter who you are, when your life becomes bigger than you, trying to explain how you feel and what you're dealing with to someone else is like trying to teach English to a Martian. That was the situation Martin was in, and there was only so much of his language I could understand because I hadn't been to Mars yet. But he did make an impression on me and gave me some advice that I remembered later on when I was going through troubles of my own. Martin told me that the only way to become man enough to deserve everything was to survive it—to do whatever it took to keep everything you'd worked hard for and achieved from getting taken away. For me that meant getting out of survival mode, which is something that most people who come from places like I'm from never do. Survival mode is a self-destructive attitude; you just take everything because you're used to barely getting by and you think it could all go away at any time. When you start to have some success, it's a real shortsighted, ignorant mentality that can keep you from planning your career properly or taking care of your money, and usually it's that kind of attitude that ends up landing newly famous people in jail or on drugs.

All of that was still a long way off for me. Back then I was making about three or four thousand dollars for my cameos on *Martin*. Once I'd finished taping each appearance and my little visit to Hollywood was over, I'd be right back on a plane to the hood. I was keeping things together and taking care of the family, but it was always a struggle and nothing was ever secure. We were in survival mode. I did club gigs to pay the rent, and being on *Martin* helped keep the lights on, for sure, but I wanted something regular that could take me to the next level.

I went back to doing stand-up full-time, which had definitely become more lucrative after having my face on a sitcom. I had a good manager by then named Barry Katz, who started to push me to do things that I would never have gone after on my own. I was comfortable in the urban comedy world, in sketches and on-stage, and I saw myself as continuing to move up that ladder, into films and other television shows. He had a different target in mind for my evolution as an artist: He got me an audition for *Saturday Night Live*. My reaction was not what he expected.

"You're fucking crazy, man!" I said. "I can't do it! That's where *Eddie* came from! I can't go up in Eddie's house. No way, I can't do it. I'm not good enough, man."

"You can do it, Tracy," Barry said. "I wouldn't do that to you if I knew you weren't good enough. And I wouldn't do it to me either—I've got a reputation to uphold. You are good enough. And they're looking for someone like you."

I went home and thought about it long and hard. Sabina and I talked about it all night and all the next day. We went over every angle: What were my chances of making it? What should I do for them in my audition? How would failure feel, and how might it affect my chances of ever getting a job on another show at NBC?

If I didn't feel ready, maybe I should wait because you get only one shot at a first impression. In the end, we decided that I had to go for it, because trying and failing is better than never trying at all—and I might never get that chance again.

"You don't want to wake up an old man wondering 'What if?' do you, baby?" Sabina said.

"I don't want to wake up *next week* wondering 'What if?' I *got* to do this."

I told myself that I was a boxer in a title match; this was my one shot at glory. I was awed just being at the NBC studios at 30 Rockefeller Center for an audition—something I never expected to do when I set out to be a comedian. Even if I never saw the inside of that building again, I'd be able to say that one time I did.

But I had to push those feelings to the back of my mind; I had to focus. I had decided that the only way I'd be okay with this audition, no matter what happened, was if I went in and was nothing but myself. I had to give them a true representation of who I was, what I was about, and what I could do. I couldn't try to be whatever I thought they wanted. Sabina and I both knew that the only way I'd ever sleep at night was if I knew that they had made their decision based on the real me.

My audition tape is on the *Saturday Night Live: The Best of Tracy Morgan* DVD, by the way. If you check it out, you'll see me as I was back in the day: a lot chubbier, a lot scruffier, just me the way I was. I did a little bit of Biscuit, wearing my beanie hat, and did a few jokes about some people I knew back then, and about my one time getting arrested as a young punk.

What happened was, this man my aunt Brenda was dating was beating on her. She was one of my favorite aunts, and she was overweight and had bad legs and diabetes, and I didn't like that this man was beating on her. So I ran to my cousin's house and got a gun with no clips or bullets, then I went and found this man and threatened him. I pointed that empty gun at his head and told him he'd better stop hitting Aunt Brenda. He called the cops on me and a few hours later they came to pick me up, at around two in the afternoon, in broad daylight, with all my neighbors watching. I was scared to death as they shook me down, cuffed me, and put me in the cop car, so once I was sitting down, I just kept farting. I blew that fucking squad car up with farts, because the night before I'd had pork and beans and franks. I was farting so bad that they had to stop the car to roll the back windows down because they didn't have electric windows on that motherfucker. What can I say? They shouldn't have taken me in. It was like I was taking the cops hostage with my gas—they could not escape.

If you want to see how much I changed once I got comfortable on television, watch the clip of me appearing on Conan that's on the DVD too, where I tell one of the same stories. I'm still me, but I'm a whole different man.

Later on I found out that the casting directors and producers didn't even want to audition me—can you believe that? Had I known, I never would have gone up there! My manager had convinced *SNL* senior producer Marci Klein to see me even after she said no. What up, Marci! I love you, girl! You know I got love for you! That's Calvin Klein's daughter right there.

Man, I don't know what kind of manager Barry is, but he knew one thing for sure: If he'd been honest with me and told me that at first they didn't want to see me, I would have sooner done a free show for the KKK than go to that audition.

African Americans have so many good reasons to blame society for the things they can't do. For years, the black man has been put down and held back and beaten around in every way. From the time he was a slave to the time he got equal rights to the first time one of his albums went triple platinum, he's been asked to be grateful for the disadvantages that have been handed to him. It's a sob story we know all too well. But it's no reason to be a statistic. You've got the right to be predictable, but you've also got the freedom to change history. Just because our forefathers were forced to walk a certain path doesn't mean every black male and female alive today must walk the same one—that's not what our ancestors fought for. Yes, there are still hurdles we've got to jump. The trick is learning how to clear them instead of giving up and sitting on the bench or tripping over them on your way to the finish line. Listen to me, if there's one thing black people can do, it's jump and run. We can win this race if y'all got the courage to get in it.

Too often, past hardships and prejudice are used as excuses. If I wanted to, I could whine about how white comics and actors get better roles than me, but you know what? I never saw it that way! If I did, where's the hope? Why even try? If I saw it that way, I never would have *tried*. If you feel defeated, you will be defeated. I kept my head in the game, not in the clouds. If you stay focused, whatever happened in the past will not hold you back because only you and I and everyone here right now on earth make the future. That's true talk.

It was easy for me not to lose focus even when I failed because one thing in my life hasn't changed—I love what I do. That's the key to life: Love what you do and take pride in it. Whether you're a garbageman or the leader of the United Nations, you'd better like it or find things you like about it. Some of the happiest people I've ever met work jobs that others might not see the value in. I think the unhappiest people in the world are that way because they either hate what they do or never figured out what it is they love to do. They end up working jobs they hate because they're chasing things like money and trophy wives. They're only in it for what that job can get them and what other people will think of them because of those prizes they have. I've met so many people who only do what they do for the money. You can't do anything just for the money if you want to be happy. I love money, everybody loves money, but if getting it makes you miserable, you won't enjoy those things you can buy half as much as those who work hard at something they enjoy. Even if they make less and can buy less and live by modest means, they'll appreciate what they have so much more. Hating your job and doing it just for the money is like winning a prize on a game show and then finding out you have to pay taxes on it that you can't afford.

I loved what I did the minute I started doing it, and I feel the same way today. I wanted to make money, sure I did; I had a family to support. But I would have been happy with just enough to pay the bills, so long as I could keep entertaining, because I love being in show business. It has never been easy, it has always been a roller-coaster, but I wouldn't trade one of those dips or curves or loop-the-loops for a quiet train ride to the promised land. I'd do it all over again the same way, with all the loss and tears and all.

Show business is no different from living on the streets, and one thing I learned on the streets is that racism is *real.* You have black people who do not like white people, you have Puerto Ricans who do not like Dominicans, and you have Jamaicans who do not like African Americans. That's America, but it's the same all over the world. Ask Europe! Don't the French hate the British? Don't all of you hate the Germans? I was never like that because my father was never like that either. Being a musician, he knew cats from all kinds of backgrounds who were brought together by their love of music. I also think that the army made him color-blind. He was in the same situation, risking his life, just trying to live another day, with dudes of all races and all walks of life from all around the country. Bullets and land mines don't see

skin color—and neither did my dad. But that's not the norm here
in this country. Racism is everywhere, even in show business. I
look at it like this: Society gave me a ten-foot wall and a five-foot
ladder and then sat back to see if I'd get my black ass over that
wall. It wasn't impossible, but I had to be creative.

I always try to keep a positive outlook on life and make positive connections with my fellow human beings. But it's gotten
harder for me to do that as my career has grown. When you're on
television, people think they know you, but they don't. They can
read every article ever written about you, but they won't ever
know what your life is like at home.

My relationships with my family, my relatives, and my friends
who stopped acting like friends once I had something they
wanted have been a drama that's taken more out of me than any
role I've ever played. All of my past hardships are nothing com-
pared with what has followed my success. That, not the struggle,
is what's broken my heart and bruised my spirit. I come from a
land of broken dreams and unfulfilled promises, and that is what
makes people hate. That desperation can make people hate those
closest to them. That has become my reality, and I see it for what
it is. It took me a long time to get here, and I almost didn't make
it. And it all started with *SNL.*

L anding a spot as a cast member on *Saturday Night Live* was a
gift from God, but like anyone who has been there can tell
you, staying there is something else altogether.

All of you would-be comedians, listen to me: If you can survive on that show, you can survive anything in the world. If you
think you know about rejection and criticism, you have no idea
until you've walked those halls. A lifetime of audition rejections
is like half a season there. How can it not be? That show is an

American institution with very high standards and a legacy no one can touch. There's only one way to keep that reputation, and that's to be *harsh*.

There's a lot of competition among the cast and the writers—everyone wants to get their skits on the air because they know what that exposure can do for their careers. *Saturday Night Live* can take you to the moon, or it can crash you out into obscurity in just one week. Check it out—the list of cast members who've faded away is much, much longer than the list of those who've gone on to bigger things.

Me? All I want at the end of the day is to have my star on the Hollywood Walk of Fame. I want to leave my mark right there, on the sidewalk, where my grandkids and my great-grandkids can visit. I want them to walk down the street one day long after I'm gone, take a picture by my star, and say, "This one here is my great-grandpop's. He got his star because Grandpop put it *in*! He put in *work*." Failure is not an option in my life. I told you already, when opportunity knocked, I pulled out the .44 Mag and said, "Get in the fucking basement, bitch!" Opportunity's still down there, ball-gagged and duct-taped up. If you listen hard, you can hear him whimper.

Being on *Saturday Night Live* is a grind, and here's how it goes: On Monday, the cast and writers have a pitch meeting in Lorne Michaels's office with that week's host. About fifty people sit around, all over the floor and the couch, and everyone gets to make two pitches. The funnier your pitch, the better the chances that one of the writers will connect with it or that Lorne will connect with it or that the whole room will approve of it. Some of the cast members might come in with a list of notes or a page or two written out, but I was never much of a writer, so at first I never showed up with more than just a rough idea. Sometimes I would have worked on it with one of the writers, sometimes it was just straight from my brain.

A lot of ideas are served up and judged at that meeting, so Mondays are full of rejection all around. But there are no visible tears because no one in that room would be there if they weren't used to rejection. I was no different; it was nothing to me. I'd been booed by the entire Apollo Theater, and I was still getting up onstage and doing it.

Whatever ideas survive the pitch meeting move on to writing day, Tuesday. Tuesday is a long day; the whole cast and writing team stay overnight. We'd take showers in the studio and spend a straight twenty-four hours creating the week's show. It's intense. Sometimes after working hours on a sketch, you start to lose sight of what's funny about it, and sometimes in the middle of those long hauls you get flashes of brilliance. It all plays out. In the meantime, you've got to stay focused.

On Wednesday there's a table reading of every single sketch that was approved and written up the day before. There are stacks and stacks of them, and getting through them all takes about five hours. Once all the sketches have been read, the head writers and the host go into Lorne's office and stay there until they've picked out which ones will make the show. While they're in there figuring it out, the cast is waiting around anxiously. At about 11 P.M., the door to Lorne's office opens and everyone finds out what sketches they're in. If your sketch is cut, you'll never hear a reason why; it just didn't make the cut. That kills a lot of people, but I never bled when it happened to me. I was like Denzel in *Glory*—I didn't cry, I didn't bleed, I stayed proud. I had a Christmas tree made of scars on my back from all the rejection I'd seen before I even set foot in the NBC studios. Losing a sketch on the show? Please, that was nothing to me. I'll never forget walking into Lorne's office on Thursdays to see the list of what was going to air. There'd be a big board in there with two columns. If a sketch is on the right, it's going to make it to the next stage and most likely see airtime; if it's on the left, it's dead and gone. In the beginning, there were many weeks when all of my sketches were on the left, but that changed as time went on.

Getting on the right side of that board doesn't mean the battle is over, though. Sketches are cut up until the last minutes, even after dress rehearsal. You never get reasons why. Sometimes the sketches that got the most laughs from the cast and writers all the way through get cut at the end, while some of the worst shit is kept in. As a cast member you might be in every skit all week long, but by the end of dress rehearsal you're only showing up at the end to say good night. Even if you make it in, you still have to hope your sketch is on before "Weekend Update," because after that, no one is watching. For years, ratings have made it very clear that by that time, people have tuned out. That time slot made people crazy! Motherfuckers would get distraught over those last few minutes of airtime. That shit got tedious.

On Thursday and Friday the cast rehearses the show, and then on Saturday it's poppin'. There's a dress rehearsal at noon, a full-dress run-through at 8 P.M., and then at 11:30 we do it live, baby. Come what may, whatever happens, it's going out there to millions of homes.

After a whole week of hard work and pressure, there's just one thing to do—party! Those after parties are infamous; I'd heard about them before I even got to SNL, and they lived up to their reputation. When I went to my first few parties, all I could think about was what they must have been like when Eddie was around. During my time, I definitely did my part to make a few of them parties times to remember. Once I got comfortable being on SNL, that was it—I got loose. Real loose.

LEFT: I'm dropping the brown shark right now.
BELOW: They don't teach photo composition in
the ghetto: me with half a head playing ring
bearer at my aunt Pat's wedding.

That's my heart: my dad, Jimmy (holding baby), my great-grandmother Nan, and me.

The Morgans: (top row, left to right) my mother, my uncle Alvin, my father, my aunt Pat, my grandfather Jimmy senior, and my aunt Niecey; (bottom row) my aunt Cynthia, my brother Jim, my great-grandmother Nan, me, my grandmother Rose, and my aunt Lorraine.

Running track
in 1985.

You didn't know I could heal white people with the touch of my hand, did you?

ABOVE: I even look fast, don't I? The track team, 1985. RIGHT: Me with Coach Bert Blanco at DeWitt Clinton High School.

Better late than never: receiving my honorary diploma and football jersey from DeWitt Clinton High School, 2002.

The best way to reach kids is to visit schools.

I'm gonna be one hot grandmother someday: me as Maya Angelou on *SNL* in 2002.

RIGHT: Me with my Obi-Wan Kenobi, Lorney Lorne Michaels. BELOW: Lorne is my Yoda, but I'm Yoda's Yoda: me imitating Sam Jackson on *SNL* in 2002.

Not quite how it really went down: on the set of *The Tracy Morgan Show,* 2003.

Me with Spoonie Luv from up above, at the premiere of *Crank Yankers,* 2002.

SNL Weekend Update with Tina Fey and Jimmy Fallon, 2003.

I know what's under your shirt, Mrs. Jackson: me as Brian Fellow on *SNL* in 2004.

I am one foxy female: with Chris Rock in *The Longest Yard,* 2005.

Ladies, control yourselves: Tracy Jordan during the *30 Rock* pilot.

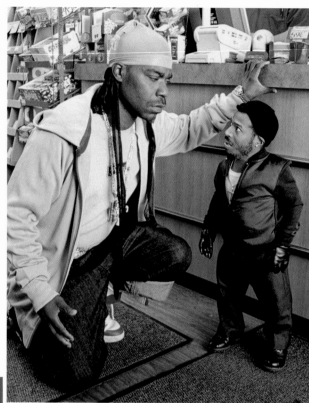

LEFT: It's amazing when actors do things like lose height for a role: me and Marlon Wayans in *Little Man*. BELOW: Alec, are we toasting to the Emmy nominations or the Golden Globes?

I look like a lesbian version of Prince: with Jane Krakowski and Lonny Ross on *30 Rock*, 2006.

The party can start now: at the Screen Actors Guild Awards with Scott Adsit (behind my hand), Grizz Chapman, Kevin Powell (behind my arm), Judah Friedlander (in the hat), me, and Kevin Brown.

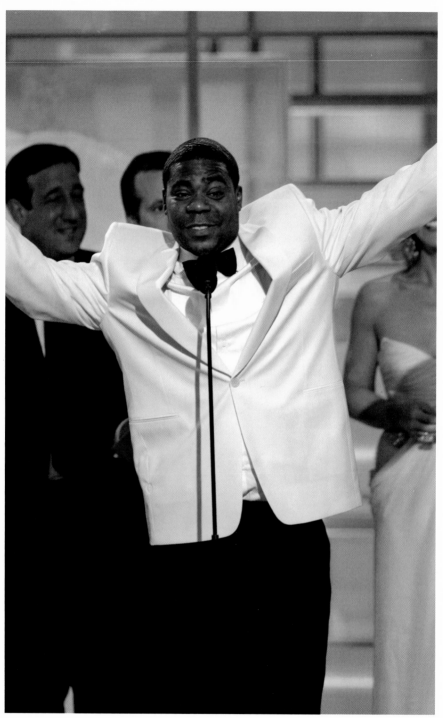

Yes we did! Giving the acceptance speech on behalf of *30 Rock* at the Golden Globes, 2009.

ABOVE: I told you I look good as a blonde: in the *Big Love* skit with Casey Wilson, Michaela Watkins, Abby Elliott, and Jason Sudeikis on the night I came back to *SNL* as host, 2009.
LEFT: Sabina and me, 2004.

My family: Gitrid, Malcolm, me, Tracy junior, and Sabina at the *Little Man* premiere, 2006.

O nce I got my first check from NBC for *Saturday Night Live,* I had enough money to move my family out of the the South Bronx, out of the ghetto, for good. We moved the day after my birthday, on November 11, 1996, at four o'clock in the morning. I celebrated my birthday at this club and restaurant, Jimmy's Bronx Café. I left when they closed, went right home—Sabina had packed us all up—and we were gone by six in the morning. Anybody who's lived in the ghetto knows that you don't move during the daytime. Here's why: You don't want anyone knowing you're leaving, and you don't want anyone knowing where you're going. You don't want anybody seeing your shit and knowing where they can get their hands on it. If they see you moving out, you can be damn sure they'll be sitting there on the sidewalk with an adding machine, totaling up how much they can get when they rob your new place. The Morgans were out of that apartment in two hours in the dead of night. No one in that neighborhood knew we were gone for at least two months.

It really was time for us to go. Forget about me being on TV and having more money; it was getting uglier in our neighborhood every day. I'm just glad we could leave before our kids got any older. In the nineties, the hood had more money coming in than ever. The economy was doing well, so there was more money at every level of society, and hip-hop had become a legitimate money-making industry by then too. But all that progress only made motherfuckers *hungrier.* No one was satisfied with being average anymore. As soon as someone saw a cat he came up with get on, he demanded the same for himself. It didn't matter that he couldn't rap like his boy could, he wanted what his boy had. That's why we got a lot of dead rappers and a lot of other dead motherfuckers too.

In the nineties, the neighbor part of our neighborhoods got capped and all that was left behind was the hood. And the hood is no place to raise a family if you've got a choice. I'm blessed to have had a choice. I wanted a better life for my family; I wanted my kids to have all the chances I never had.

We moved to Riverdale, which is still in the Bronx, but a whole world away. The first thing I noticed was that white people don't think sidewalks are trash cans! It was the first time I'd seen clean pavements in my life! And there were people walking on it, smiling, just going for a stroll. I'd never gone on a walk for no reason, with no destination, in my entire life. I tried it, just walking around, taking in the sights, and I realized it was pretty nice. It relaxed me, much more than it relaxed all the nice Jewish people I smiled at whenever I toured the neighborhood. They would check their pockets and look around for cops when they saw me, but that didn't bother me. I just smiled at them as wide as I could. I wasn't going to let them make me feel funny. I was going to make sure they felt funny for trying to make me feel funny. Does that make sense to you? It should! Hi, nice Jewish people! It's a beautiful day! I'm black and I live next to you!

In all seriousness, it was a major culture shock for me and my family. We got some evil looks from our neighbors, and school was much different for the kids. But we just looked at ourselves as the Jeffersons, moving on up whether the neighbors liked it or not. It was the first time, but not the last, that my home life and my work life went through big transitions at the same time. Sabina and I were learning new things, but episodes in our lives didn't end with laughs and a lesson learned. At home we were figuring out what it meant to live in a white neighborhood, and at work I was figuring out what it meant to live in white comedy. It took me about two days to realize that white funny ain't just black funny in makeup. I knew I was going to have to find my place at home and at work. I was on a planet I'd never visited before, and I did not know the customs of these aliens.

I showed up at *SNL* with a lifetime of ghetto experience and years of making it happen in the world of black comedy. I came from *Def Jam,* from *Martin,* from appearances on *Live at the Apollo* and in black-oriented comedy clubs around the country. Everyone I knew had stopped watching *SNL* when Eddie Murphy left—and that meant me too. That is probably why Marci and Lorne brought me in, because I'm real-life ghetto. Choosing me for the cast was like giving white America a dose of BET. But *SNL* wasn't ready for that, not at first, that's for sure. They must have known they wanted a part of it, but they didn't know what it really meant. It took a while for us to get used to each other.

Four months after I got into stand-up professionally I was on TV, and that was because there were so many urban vehicles for black comedy at the time that are now long gone. I was part of a movement and a community and a moment. Put it this way: I used to do routines as fat Michael Jackson from the projects, and they killed wherever I went. I made fun of the tragedy of the ghetto and was used to audiences who found that funny. I had my finger on the pulse of urban comedy, but when I brought my act to *SNL,* those motherfuckers just felt bad for me. None of the cast I came up with saw this future for me. No, sir. All I have to say about that is, where's Chris Kattan now? Where's Cheri Oteri now? That bitch can't even get arrested. None of them laughed at Biscuit when I did him then, but if I did it for them now, I bet you a million they'd say it's funny. It's all right; I don't mind. It's hard to get mainstream America to catch up. Mainstream America has just learned the words to Sugarhill's "Rapper's Delight"! And we don't do that shit no more! Jay-Z and Lil Wayne don't sound like that! No one sounds like that no more!

Making a place for myself in the *SNL* scheme took some time.

I knew the score; this was a white show and I was the token black guy. That didn't bother me; I was used to those odds. Of course Will Ferrell fit in every sketch they'd ever come up with, but not me. That's just how it was, so my answer to that was being as funny as a motherfucker whenever I got the ball. Those weeks when my sketches made it to air, I made sure those minutes belonged to *me*. I didn't care who was in my sketch, I was going to eat their lunch! I was out to steal their thunder. When I got my shot at the basket, I drove the lane and dunked. I'd sink threes from the baseline and bring those rebounds down throwing elbows left and right. I was going to win; I didn't care how.

It didn't matter to me if I only had a one-line drive-by or an entire sketch. It didn't matter if it was the first sketch of the night or the very last one that no one even watches. I gave it everything I had, every time. And eventually people took notice of me. In the pitch meetings, people started to pay more attention to what I had to say. The writers started to connect with my ideas and take the time to write them up. I found my way into the system through patience and perseverance.

When I started getting regular airtime and feeling like I was part of the team, my *SNL* world changed. I was still coming from somewhere different, but I started to team up with a few of the writers, and for the first time I understood what it meant to collaborate. That's a whole other form of creativity that stand-up cannot teach you. Writing with someone is very rewarding when you both see eye to eye. A rough idea that's halfway funny can blossom into full-blown funny within just a few minutes if it's bounced off the right minds. This realization opened up new ways for me to think about comedy, and with that advantage on my side, the writers and I started to come up with regular characters.

Once you develop recurring characters, *Saturday Night Live* becomes the show Lorne designed it to be: a showcase for emerging comic talent. The first big character of mine that became a regular was Brian Fellow. One night, Sabina and I were lying in bed and she was telling me about this gay guy she knew in high school named Fellow. I never met him, but what you see in the character is what I took from her description. I was cracking up just listening to her talk about him, so I knew there was something there I could use. I brought it in to *SNL* and pitched him.

"Here's something I want to do," I said. "It's a guy named Brian Fellow. He's like this . . ." I started acting gay and everyone laughed. "I'm Brian Fellow *and you're not*!" I kept saying.

I said he was this weird gay dude who imagined stuff in his head and thought he knew everything. My man Tim Herlihy picked right up on that shit. (Tim writes for Adam Sandler, by the way.) He saw a bigger picture. I don't know where he got the idea, but he thought Brian Fellow should host an animal talk show. That sent the room into hysterical laughter. A delusional gay guy interviewing animals? What the fuck is that, Tim? I loved it, I knew it was gold, but I had to look at Tim and say, "What is *wrong* with you, dude?"

Tim and I got to work on writing it up, and the first thing we did was record the theme song to the show, which we named *Brian Fellow's Safari Planet*. If I thought it was a good idea before, now I knew it was a hit. It takes a lot to make me think something is weird, so when I do, I know it's hilarious. Brian Fellow is a gay, self-centered, paranoid host of an *animal talk show*. And he only has a sixth-grade education too. The best thing about Brian's sketches was the voice-overs—that's where I could show how insane he really was. Brian worries about animals stealing his wallet and credit cards. He worries about animals talking shit about him. He's ridiculous! That character allowed me to say things that were nothing but completely absurd.

Another one of my regular characters was Woodrow. He was my first attempt at playing tragedy and comedy at the same time, which is something I always thought Eddie Murphy did so well on *SNL*. Eddie's character Mister Robinson was funny as hell, but he was also sad; when he joked about being poor and avoiding Mr. Landlord, the message beneath the surface was real. Mister Robinson's situation was like too many everyday people's, which made the comedy a little bit uncomfortable to watch.

That kind of humor was nothing new; it was the formula Richard Pryor invented and lived better than anyone ever will. He's the ultimate; the rest of us are just paying tribute. When I came up with Woodrow, it was my chance to pay tribute to Richard and Eddie in some small way. I wanted him to be an evolution of what Eddie had done on *SNL,* but sadder and stranger. So I thought: "What's worse than living in the ghetto? That's easy—living in a sewer!"

Woodrow became my version of Oscar the Grouch. In every skit he would almost succeed, but in the end he would always fail at getting the girl, usually played by an attractive female host. Woodrow was the saddest clown I could imagine. He was never getting out of the sewer and he was never getting anything he wanted, no matter how close he came. I saw him as being in the same category as the more socially conscious comedy that *SNL* did back in the seventies. Go back and watch it all; you'll see what I'm talking about.

Another character I enjoyed getting on the air regularly was Dominican Lou. He was my way of letting all Americans know that Dominicans are here and they're not going anywhere. If America wasn't going to hire them, I sure as hell was going to play one because I grew up around them. He was my salute to the Dominican nation in this diverse town we call New York. Dominican Lou was the superintendent of an apartment building who

thought he owned the place just because he had the keys to every
door. He's the kind of character who would stand outside the
building with a can of beer and tell you you couldn't park in front
because it was his spot and his building. He was the kind of guy
who you would see every day for five years but if you asked him
to let you into the building because you forgot your keys, he'd say,
"Who you? You no live heeere." Lou's funny like that.

For me, *Saturday Night Live* was like being Alice in Wonder-
land. I was out of place from the start, and the further down
that rabbit hole I fell, the more fantastic the ride became. The
show consumed all of my creativity, and I loved it. Every week
there was variety, and not knowing what was around the corner
kept it fresh for me. It kept me learning; it kept me on my toes.

But that wasn't the only thing that kept me alert. Being the
black guy on the show put me in a different category, in my mind
at least. Like I said, I couldn't mess around. I felt like any mistake
I made might be my last. I didn't feel like I had the freedom to
blunder. Look in the books—there have never been a lot of black
guys on *SNL,* and there still aren't. I believe that even today, on
mainstream shows, outside of the urban television market, black
people on TV are held to a higher standard. I certainly felt that
way on *SNL.* I never thought it would be okay for me to break
character like Jimmy Fallon and all of them did. That thought
never crossed my mind, because I would have seen it as a failure
on my part, and I thought others might see it that way too.

It's funny, I look back on some of the shows that inspired me
and inspired so many comedy writers, from the best of them, like
Tina Fey, to the guys in the trenches coming up, and they are the
complete opposite of what flies for mainstream television comedy
today. The shows that inspired me were things like *Sanford and*

Son and *Good Times* and *Diff'rent Strokes.* If a network put a show like any of those on today, the NAACP would be all over them. They'd have a landslide lawsuit on their hands. Think about *Diff'rent Strokes:* a show about two black kids from Harlem being raised by an old white guy. The politically correct nation we have become would find that wrong twenty-four ways to Sunday. The truth is, everybody is too sensitive today. That PC shit is killing comedy. And that's why I love being on *30 Rock.* I'm jumping ahead, but you want to know the moment when I knew we had a hit on our hands? When I read the script for the episode in the first season called "The C Word," which was about sensitivity training. Tina's got balls, because we did a whole show about saying the word *nigger*! And it was bleeped out on purpose, but we all said it during the filming, and you could read our lips. We need to get back to the days of Archie Bunker, when they openly made fun of racism. That's healthy if you ask me. We are living in an age where someone like Michael Jackson went so far to show us that we're all the same inside that he changed his fucking skin color.

Anyway, after a while, I fell in with a few great writers at *SNL* who understood me more than anyone else had, and they made my career by giving me the chance to shine. They saw my range, and more important, they taught me to stretch it. I have to thank T. Sean Shannon and Andrew Steele, my dark horses, who got me before anyone else did. I hooked up with those two, and they gave me the material that showcased my funny. So did Paula Pell and, of course, Tina Fey. Once Tina and I got together, it was over. Tina wasn't scared to come into my world and find the funny up in there. She's that kind of cool. Tina Fey, you know most of all what you did for me. Look at me, Tina Fey! I have to say it now and I'll say it again: I LOVE YOU, GIRL. I will always rock with you because you know my voice better than I do sometimes.

At SNL we were all definitely a family. It was competitive, but there was a camaraderie that everyone was a part of. It was very special to me, working there. It wasn't like *The Waltons* or *The Brady Bunch,* and we didn't have pajama parties or hang out like it was a dorm, but we did have a kind of family. And the head of it was my Obi-Wan Kenobi, Lorne Michaels. He gave me my shot at real, national fame, and how much I owe him is self-explanatory. He changed my life and my kids' lives. They say that every Jewish man has got to love one nigger in his life. I'm glad Lorne Michaels chose me.

To tell you the truth, I wasn't really friends with many of my castmates at *SNL*, but that doesn't mean that I didn't roll up into *SNL* and all those after parties with my own friends. My time on *SNL* marked the beginning of my days rolling with an entourage that was much, much too big. I'd go out with about thirty people when I could. I used to come up in every club surrounded by felons. I had this felon named Young God around me, I had Pumpkin, I had motherfuckers named Guilty all around me. And I always brought D. Nice, who was just straight trouble. The rest of the cast never fucked with me. I can't imagine why.

One time, though, I did get a lot of them to come to an after party that friends of mine were throwing. If you're a fan of *30 Rock* and you've seen the episode where Liz Lemon goes out all night with Tracy Jordan and follows him to the After-After-After-After Party, this night is where Tina got all that from.

Friends of mine were running this illegal strip club they called the Loft. It was in an office space they'd rented and converted into an after-the-after-party spot. They put a stage in it, they put a few futons all around, and they'd get strippers and girls to come and do shows. You'd walk in there and get your dick sucked, there was usually some fucking going on, and there was liquor and couches everywhere. But this place was just a regular apartment space, so the bar was really just the kitchen, and there was only one bathroom, which usually got stopped up at some point because of all kinds of shit getting stuffed in there. I invited everyone to go down there one week. And Tina Fey, Rachel Dratch, and a few others came along.

I didn't tell any of them what they were in for, so it was all cool when we got there. At first, as they got their drinks and sipped them and talked, they thought it was just a private party. Then these two girls came out onstage and started going down on each other and that just shut it *down*. All the grips and crew guys from *SNL* were standing around and loving it, but my castmates took one look at that, turned right around, and rushed out of there. They were all a bunch of Ivy League faggots and we'd taken it to the streets. They might have left, but it was all that anybody talked about around the show for the next week. None of them ever came back, but me and my boys did it for another two weeks at least.

Actually, one cast member really got into it. This party started late and kept going strong right into the morning. The next day around noon, I got a call from the guy running the party.

"Yo, Tray, what's up?"

"Nothing. I'm getting some rest," I said. "What's goin' on?"

"Yo, I can't get your man to leave."

"What are you talking about?" I asked. "Who? D. Nice?"

"No, man, the fat guy from your show!"

"Who? *Horatio?*"

"Yeah, man, that's him," he said. "He's still here. He's sitting on a couch with two girls. He's been smoking a cigar and just talking to them for hours. He's the only one here, man, and he won't leave."

Being on *Saturday Night Live* made me addicted to fame. And that is the worst drug known to man. I got hooked on the "oohs" and "aahs," and once I did, I did whatever it took to chase them. On- and offstage, in and out of work, I needed that attention. Having cameras around didn't even matter to me after a while; once I was somewhat known—not even full-blown famous—I had to be the center of everyone's attention no matter where I was.

Fame will twist your vision. All of a sudden, I was that naïve kid back on set at *Martin,* scared to death that I'd fail unless I made everyone laugh all the time. And just like I did back then, I turned to the bottle and used alcohol to keep my confidence up and my crazy level high. Drinking became my free pass to entertain wherever I was, 24–7. I wasn't an alcoholic; I kept liquor and champagne in my house for years without touching it, because I didn't need it at home. I never even thought about it there. But when I was out, which was every night, I needed my drinks.

The more of a television personality I became—someone everyone in the audience thought they knew—the more I felt I had a character to play, even in my real life. In my mind, my importance and my fame depended on making sure I did what people expected of me. I was famous, wasn't I? I'm Tracy Morgan! I'm a comedian and I'm on TV! I'm supposed to be out at the clubs all night every night, right? Dancing more than you because I have more fun than anybody does! That's the kind of thing I was telling myself every night after my third vodka and juice.

Everyone was drinking, so I had to drink more. I'd ball with bottles every time I came through the door. If I didn't, I wasn't succeeding at being this entertainer called Tracy Morgan. I had to be *on* in public, I had to be as insane as I ever was on TV *and* be myself at the same time. I wanted to live out loud and advertise my success. Lots of Belvedere vodka, preferably drunk straight from the bottle, was the best way to get to that place. I wasn't going to be anything less than a spectacle when I stepped out in a club.

After too many afternoons waking up with a hangover, not even sure how I got home at all, I just got tired of it. It was played out to me. I looked in the mirror and just grew up. Well, not really. I grew up for a minute and stopped that shit. And then I forgot that moment of clarity and dove headfirst into the whirlpool again. The second time I learned my lesson because I got the message loud and clear: If I kept on living like that, I'd die, and I'd probably kill someone on the way. You can't get high without coming down. It's a simple idea even a child can understand. But that don't make it any easier when it happens. It took two DUIs and being strapped with an ankle bracelet, plus having to face a list of health problems I'd tried to ignore, to get me to pay attention, all while I enjoyed the greatest success I'd ever known.

BLACK COMEDY IS
Eddie Murphy

Eddie works with the honesty of Richard and Redd, but he knows how to do it without exposing too much of himself. He took the greatest elements of that head-on comedy and used them to become a rock star. He came from the same school as them, got the same degree, but it was twenty years later, a time when there were more jobs. If Richard was like a vice president of Xerox, Eddie was like the CEO of Apple. Every comedian who gets paid $20 million a movie owes it to Eddie. He made it possible for a comedian to be a pop icon, hands down. And he deserves it—he's go so much talent, from the singing, to his impersonations, to his acting. He can do it all.

CHAPTER 5

The Tracy Morgan Show

'm somewhere I never thought I'd be. I'm in my forties, I'm comfortable, and I'm proud of myself. I'm a good father, I'm an independent man, I've got money, and I didn't have to do a nickel or a dime in the penitentiary to get here. I've already done more than I ever expected—and I'm just getting started.

I still have many goals in life, but there is one I think I can reach without a struggle now that I've got my mind and my body straight: I just want my forties to be good. I want them to be calm, productive, healthy—just *good.* My thirties were turbulent. They were like flying through a lightning storm on the way to spring break in Cancún: You're having fun because you're already partying on your way to an even bigger party, but you're getting tossed all over the place, you're about to throw up your Hennessy all over some girl, and there's a chance your plane might crash. The ups and downs in my thirties wore me *out*. Part of it was youth, but at the time I thought all that action was what it meant to be a success in show business. In my mind, it was proof of success, a status symbol, like a platinum chain on a rapper. It didn't matter if that guy spent his whole album advance on that thing— he has to have it if he wants to ball. I thought being famous meant I was supposed to be at the center of that kind of storm; it was proof that I had the skills to pay the bills.

Now that I'm older and wiser, I realize that's bullshit. You can be known all the world over and still have a normal, fulfilling home life. You don't have to be a nightclub Superman. You can do the best work of your life as an entertainer without all of the madness. That shit is just a distraction, anyway—none of it inspires you or feeds your talent. Just because someone acts entitled, like they should be treated as someone special, doesn't mean that they are.

Normal celebrities exist, but they're mighty rare. If you only look at the universe of gossip websites and TV shows to comprehend the nature of American celebrity, you would think that normal celebrities are mythical creatures like unicorns and leprechauns. You don't usually hear about the entertainers who live quietly, away from the paparazzi. Instead you hear about the ones who crash cars while cheating with tranny hookers. Why the media treats every celebrity fuckup like it's the first time somebody famous has behaved that way mystifies me. Doesn't anyone see a pattern here? Celebrities need attention fixes, and people pay attention to outrageous behavior, so celebrities get outrageous. That's what it is at its most basic; once you add the psychology of being creative to the mix, you've got all kinds of motives to act out.

But it's not just celebrities—look at reality television. Regular people are willing to do anything to get their fifteen minutes of fame these days. They'll eat garbage to win a jar of peanut butter

on some show where the prize money won't last them a year after taxes. Girls will get naked and cover themselves in meat if some washed-up rock star tells them to on VH1. A lot of people would rather do anything than work hard, and they see fame as an easy way to do nothing, so they chase it like drug dealers chase paper. The kind of easy fame that comes from reality TV has made fame crackheads out of people who might have had a normal life, and it's made people without talent think they can be stars. When a person who wants to be famous gets famous, no one should be surprised when that person gets crazy. Handing fame to someone like that is like giving a drug addict your bank card and PIN. You'd better change your address and close your account, because you've got a fucked-up situation on your hands.

Listen, we're all free to do what we want with our lives— celebrities even more so because if they've got a decent career, they've got enough money to buy freedom. But living crazy don't make you talented. Living crazy on television just makes you a clown and a footnote. It makes you a YouTube video that no one will remember in a year. Talent is something else; it comes from *inside you.* It is a gift given to you by God, but it's up to you to use it. You have to *nurture* it; you can't just wait for your talent to work its magic on your own and make everything in your life okay. You have to work to perfect it. You may think crazy behavior is expected of famous people, but if you live life to fulfill other people's expectations, you're not even living. You're dead. You're a fucking zombie and a robot.

I look back on my turbulent thirties like I'm looking at pictures from someone else's spring break. Some of those pictures are dirty too! I learned a valuable lesson in those days: When you're seventeen, you think you know it all; when you're twenty-five, you know you know it all; when you're thirty-five, you think you'll do it all; and when you're forty, you finally realize the truth—*you don't know shit!* That's the greatest knowledge a man can have. Once every man accepts it, our world will be a better place. It's a big world, and if you go through it feeling like you know nothing, you'll be ready to learn something each and every day you're alive.

When you're on TV, people demand things from you, and last time I checked, life for the average person was already pretty fucking demanding. When you're on TV, people act like a girl who turns to you in bed and says, "Make me come. Right now! Make me come!" You're there, you're chilling. You've already done it with her, and you're enjoying some peace and quiet. You're like a sports car that's been taken out on the highway and put back in the garage. When a woman turns to me like that, I snap right back: "Girl, how the fuck am I going to make you come if you're not willing to do that shit on your own?" I'm no monster, we can collaborate on it, you know, but there's something everyone's got to realize, no matter what the situation is: I get *paid* to perform! And after I've given it my all, especially after putting in a long week on set, I sure as hell don't want to put in an encore performance at home in bed. Ladies, you must understand this.

I have a rule for my life: I don't demand anything I can't get myself. I think everybody should follow the same rule, whether we're talking about orgasms or dollar bills. I just want to be paid what I deserve for my work. Demanding what you don't deserve and you can't get yourself? That's rude. As long as I meet my audience's expectations, I'm doing my job, wherever I am.

Let's get back to my story. You'll see why I had to get all that stuff off my chest, because the period of my life after *SNL* was when all of those themes played out in my biopic.

When I decided to leave *Saturday Night Live* in 2003, I was taking the chance I had to take. By then, Will Ferrell had left, Molly Shannon had left, and I was one of the only ones left from the class I came up with. New people started joining the cast, and even though I was at the top of the food chain, I got the feeling that I had to move on.

I could easily have stayed there, but I didn't want to be one of those guys who hung around too long. For damn sure I didn't want to be one of those motherfuckers who just disappeared forever. I'll never forget my little sister, Asia, telling me after I'd been on the show for a while, "You've got to promise me something. Don't be there *too* long, Tracy. Keep challenging yourself and trying new things. Don't get too comfortable." That was hard to hear coming from my little sister, but she was right. She knew that sometimes people on *SNL* stay too long and get scared of taking a chance on anything else because they're used to the money. When they finally leave, they have no idea what to do to get that kind of guaranteed paycheck elsewhere, and often their moment has passed. I wasn't any different, but I wasn't scared. It had been a nice run, but it was time to grow up and leave Daddy's house. In the end I left right on time, in my lucky number seventh year.

Doors had started opening for me thanks to *Saturday Night Live,* but I was no Eddie Murphy or Adam Sandler. I wasn't an easy fit for the movies. Six years later motherfuckers are just now realizing who I am and what to do with me. I always tell people that it took fifteen or sixteen years for it to happen for me overnight, so maybe in fifty years people will still be figuring out how to use my talents in this business. God is never there when we want Him to be, but He's always right on time. You must have faith, but you've got to meet Him halfway. If you think my success happened by chance, you probably believe Rick Ross was really a gangbanger. Man, I wish Biggie was still around—he'd have put the Dirty South on hold for at least ten years. Rick Ross would still be a corrections officer eating Swanson's TV dinners.

In my last year at *SNL,* I started thinking about what I wanted to do next, and I realized I wanted to do my own TV show. So I developed the idea for *The Tracy Morgan Show.* It was a sitcom based on the time when my brother Paris, my sister, Asia, and I lived with our father, Jimmy, and our stepmom, Gwen. My whole family is funny as hell; I'm not the only one who's got it, so I planned to draw situations and characters from my early family life. Most of the Morgans are all the good kind of crazy in their own way, so I had a lot to work with.

The formula for the show was perfect: It would be true-life funny set against the realistic backdrop of a low-income household like the one I was raised in. Imagine *Married with Children* and *Roseanne* mixed up with *What's Happening!!* and *Sanford and Son.* The idea as I pitched it was good, so it got picked up by NBC while I was heading into the last half of my final season on *SNL.* Lorne Michaels signed on as executive producer, and we were ready to roll.

By my second year at *SNL* I was feeling like my manager, Barry Katz, had taken me as far as he could; I needed a new team. When I did *The Chris Rock Show* in its first season, I met Dave Miner, a manager with 3 Arts Entertainment, and that was it. I liked him, and I felt like he could take me to the next level. Miner and his partner, Dave Becky, courted me for about a week, and then I signed on with the company. They are still with me today. They built me up and prepared me to handle my own sitcom and everything that's come since then. But even when we landed the sitcom deal, I still wasn't satisfied.

"You've got your own show, Tracy. What more do you want?" they'd ask me.

"Another zero at the end of my check."

"That will happen eventually; you have to trust us."

They were right in the end, but it was a long ride to get here.

It's been nonstop too. We went almost directly from *SNL* into preproduction on *The Tracy Morgan Show*. We shot it on the NBC lot in Los Angeles, so I had to move my wife and kids across the country just weeks after I stopped working in studio 8H at 30 Rock. That wasn't an easy transition for the Morgans.

My kids didn't want to leave their friends, and Sabina hated L.A. from the minute the plane touched down. The weather was nice but she didn't care; sunshine and swimming pools meant nothing to her. Everyday living out there was just too different for us. We weren't used to getting into a car every time we needed a roll of toilet paper. Traffic was a whole other animal. We'd seen traffic living in the Bronx—every time there was a home game at Yankee Stadium, it was bumper-to-bumper. But that shit is like a slow traffic day in Los Angeles, where people sit in their cars for hours, barely moving, just to get to work. You spend half of your day in a car trying to get somewhere—usually more time than you ever spend wherever it is you're going. Sabina wanted none of that. And it wasn't just the inconveniences; she wanted to leave L.A. because it was too artificial for her. I got love for L.A. because L.A. got love for me. I had my reason to be there, but Sabina didn't fit in and she didn't want to. She didn't want to see our kids grow up there either. It didn't help that I had to go right to work and couldn't be around so we could all adjust to it together. For some reason she misses it now; she still lives in New York but always talks about going out to the West Coast again. I think if our youngest son wasn't happy in school here, she'd probably take her divorce settlement and move out there. It's a sure sign of how much Sabina has changed since then.

My professional life also required getting used to. Even with my own show on NBC, Los Angeles was no cakewalk. I had a great paycheck and a chance at being a prime-time star, but around the studio I was the new kid in town, and I wasn't anything like the other kids. A lot of the comedians I met felt like I didn't deserve to be the star of a sitcom—and I'm talking about the supporting cast of my own show! Some of them didn't even try to hide it. Their attitude was that they'd been out there struggling, trying to get on a network production for years, and there I was flying in from New York, already on top of the heap. I wasn't part of the L.A. comedy scene, and I had everything they wanted. I'd hear them talking about it right there in the hallways and in the dressing rooms next to mine. Encountering jealousy and backstabbing like that on my own set was very discouraging. But that was only the beginning.

In the end, *The Tracy Morgan Show* that aired wasn't even my show anymore. The producers took it out of my hands because they thought that my original vision was going to damage my career—at least, that's what they told me. They also reminded me that they had more experience in this than I did. It was just like what the Republicans tried to do to Obama during the election; all they kept talking about was his lack of experience. This society is just not used to seeing black people in positions of power. No one has the experience of being a president until he is one. Unless we're talking about an election where both candidates have been president before, that is a ridiculous argument. There's an element of trust involved; you have to look at the candidate and make a leap of faith. The people who doubted me didn't believe in that.

But that's how it goes down on TV a lot of the time. There are so many people in power who put in their two cents and change things, and a lot of the time those people are the least creative links in the chain. They don't understand the show they've got; they're

out of touch with the world and insulated by the bubble of the entertainment industry. They base their decisions on marketing and
test groups, and doing that makes everything predictable and safe.
I tried to fight for my original vision, to keep the spirit of it alive,
but everyone was against me. After a while, I just gave up.

The show's creators, Jim O'Doherty and David Israel, turned
it into a false idea of what it's like to be a black family. Instead of
keeping the focus on my life growing up, which was poor and
tough but full of laughs and love, they shifted it to my present-
day life. My television family became a more middle-class family
dealing with everyday ordinary shit. The humor was average at
best, and the situations were very familiar—there was nothing in
it that hadn't been done in white shows *and* black shows a million
times before. *The Tracy Morgan Show* became a modernized
Cosby Show, where the father was a mechanic instead of a doctor.
That was not my idea at all. The last thing I wanted to do was try
to find humor in my adult home life; that story was just happening. I wanted to tell a story about the past, because that's what I
knew. I wanted to tell a story about the ghetto. There was no way
these two visions for the show could coexist. Jim O'Doherty
didn't know what the fuck he was doing, and he didn't bother to
ask me my thoughts.

We shot the eighteen episodes the network ordered. After sixteen of them aired, NBC pulled it. No one from our production
even told me. Here's how I found out: I was waiting for the show
to come on one night and a fucking infomercial came on instead.
The next day I got a call from my managers and learned the
truth. I felt like I was the only one who wasn't surprised when the
show got canceled. All these white people had no idea what they
did wrong and why their formula didn't work. I'll tell you why:
Because they don't know what it's like to be black!

That's show business, and it's gotten even worse since then.

There are so many forms of entertainment for people on the Internet today that networks and movie studios don't know what to do. They put out all that reality programming because people never seem to get tired of seeing other people doing dumb shit or living some life that's worse than their own. And when it comes to sitcoms and dramas, they throw shit up against the wall just to see if it sticks. If you stick right off the bat, you stick. If you don't, you're gone and never mentioned again.

The only way to survive is to stay on top of your team. I learned that early, back when I was just looking to book stand-up gigs outside of the Bronx. Managers and agents have many careers to look after, but you've only got one. I stay on top of everyone working for me to make sure they're doing everything they can to keep me on top. If an agent tells you they're going to take a chance on you, it's bullshit—you're the one taking a chance on *him*. If you find one you think has your back, you might spend a few years listening to his advice, following his orders, going on auditions, and taking meetings, trusting that he understands the game and how you're gonna win it. Then maybe one of his other clients lands a role that you could have done and you see your agent spend all his time milking that success. Or maybe one day you finally realize that he hasn't done enough for your career and none of those promises came true, but eventually you see what's what—that agent just kept you around in case someone wanted you. The sad truth is that by the time you figure that out, your time might have passed. That agent sat on his ass while your big break passed you by.

Look, I've got no interest in diversifying. I just want to do what I do. People tell me all the time: "You should open a club!" or "You should open a few barbershops!" Why the fuck would I do that? That's not my talent. I'm a comedian. What do I know about running a club? Getting kicked out of one—that I know how to do. I see no point in doing a lot of different things because there's no way you'll be good at all of them. Do one thing and do it the best you can. Look at Michael Jordan. He wasn't a bad baseball player, but he was the greatest at basketball, the game he was born to play. And it didn't take him long to go back where he belonged. If God gives you a talent, you've got to honor it by giving it your undivided attention.

'm not gonna lie: I was hurt when *The Tracy Morgan Show* got canceled because even though they fucked it up, it still was my show and had my name on it. If it had been called *Black Mechanic and the Funny Kids,* it might have been easier for me to take. Even though the result was so far from the original intention, when all was said and done the show was all right. But the ratings worked against us, and that's all the network people saw. All they cared about was how many people were watching and who those people were. The problem was they aimed my show at an audience it was never going to get. The show I originally planned would have entertained people in the cities, from down-south Louisiana to up-north Detroit. But the producers wanted to make all the white people in the Midwest laugh, so they made it into a parody of a black family that they would recognize. That's not my character, that's not how I get down, and my heart just wasn't in it.

So that was it for my TV show. End of story. I went back to what I knew; I hit the road to pay the bills. I stayed out there for about four years, and in that time everything changed for the Morgan family once again. We stayed in L.A. and got a bit more used to it, but we still weren't happy; we just weren't in our element. And though I love stand-up, professionally I was yearning for something more.

Around this time I met Bradley Lewis, who became my joke

writer for a while. He's a great talent—he does stand-up too. I met him in front of the Comedy Store, and we clicked right away. We have chemistry to this day; whenever we are around each other we just make each other laugh. What's up, Brad! Nothing but love, baby.

Life on the road took its toll on me, and once again I started partying full speed. When you feel like you've got nothing to lose and you spend most of your life on the road just to support a family that you hardly ever get to see, you lose sight of reality. You forget your commitments, you forget your roots, you forget your purpose. Whether you're a musician or a comedian, when you're on the road, you don't think of the past or the future after a while—you only think about what you're doing that day, that night. I indulged in everything that came my way.

That was when things began to fall apart in my marriage. Feeling that relationship slip out from under me made me even more desperate and out of control. If Sabina would have agreed to it, I would have found a way for her to be with me on the road all the time. But we couldn't do that. We had a family, we had kids in school; I couldn't drag everyone along with me to every show. That wouldn't have been any kind of life for them. Sabina likes her home and her comfort, and she likes to have her friends and loved ones around her. She had no interest in hotel rooms, comedy clubs, and airplanes. But I had to marry the road to keep us living. If you're out there too long, you get so used to it that you become uncomfortable when you're home. And once that happens, that second marriage has got you; the road becomes your number one girl. The road is nothing but groupies coming around, and there you are, in a hotel all by yourself more nights per year than you're home with your family. Shit happens. If it happened to Ray Charles, it was damn sure happening to Tracy Morgan.

Every comedy club is a free party if you're the comedian. Booze, drugs, women, whatever you want, it's there. But being back in the clubs was different than it used to be, and I didn't like it. After being on *SNL* for seven years, the people I met knew who I was and thought they knew shit about me. That scared me to death. When I'm onstage or on TV, I might be the biggest clown you ever saw, but when I'm not, I like my privacy. I've got a complicated home life and a tricky situation with my extended family, and how that all works out is nobody's business but my own. I also like cooling out with my friends just like everybody else—it's the only time I can be myself, without anyone expecting anything of me.

I had been on television so long that when I was in a club hanging out, people would come at me like they knew me personally. It was one thing if they were fans telling me they liked something I did, but that wasn't always the case. Some of them came at me trying to get what they could from me. The road got bumpy, but I had to get through it. Stand-up was all I had going aside from a few film walk-ons here and there; it was my bread and butter.

Still hurting from losing my show, I found many different medicines on the comedy circuit. I never drank before my sets, but I always made up for it afterward. Every night I was out there playing hard, even though I should have been on the bench. I'd been diagnosed with type 2 diabetes in 1996, so I had no business drinking so much and thinking an insulin shot would take care of everything. I learned about the diabetes when I woke up one day unable to see. My eyes were open, but I saw nothing at all, just black. I thought I was going blind. Sabina rushed me to the hospital and discovered that I'd been living all that time in need of regular insulin shots. My diet and everything else was starting to close up my blood vessels, including the ones in my eyes.

Again, I was ignorant of anything but survival mode. I had just gotten on *Saturday Night Live,* and the last thing I was going to let hinder me was some disease. I never took the time to learn about diabetes at all; as soon as the doctor said it wasn't deadly, I just went and forgot about it. I never bothered getting any regular medication for it, I paid no attention to what a diabetic should and shouldn't eat, and I didn't stay disciplined about taking insulin. When I felt sick every once in a while, I'd shoot myself up. I was stupid and I was doing serious damage to my body. But as long as I got through the day and got to work, I figured I was healthy enough.

I have only really learned to take care of myself properly recently, over a decade after I first found out about my condition. I spent too many years thinking I knew best, paying attention to my mind and not my body. The symptoms of my disease had been there long before I was diagnosed; I'd just gotten used to them. I'd get tired, I'd get moody, I had pains in my legs and headaches—but wasn't that normal for someone living the life of a stand-up comedian? I never thought drinking was a problem because I didn't bother to learn how much sugar was in vodka and champagne and beer. Ask any doctor or any diabetic; drinking was the worst thing I could have been doing. All that liquor put my blood sugar on a roller-coaster and seriously stressed my organs. I'm telling you, a couple of vodkas and juice to a diabetic is like freebasing coke to a normal person. It really sends you up and down. At the time I liked the feeling, I was wiling out. I just thought that's what everybody felt when they were drunk. What I've realized since is that I probably had no problems with the disease as a young man because I was an athlete. If drinking is one of the worst things a diabetic can do besides eating a whole jar of honey or drinking a bottle of maple syrup, then regular, vigorous exercise is the best thing he can do. All that training kept my condition from hurting me, until I stopped. Then the symptoms started to creep into my life.

During those three or four years after I left *The Tracy Morgan Show,* I almost slipped into a diabetic coma twice—I got real close. What I didn't know is that most people who go into a diabetic coma never come out. I don't remember much of those days because I was so sick that I had to be hospitalized and stabilized with IV medications for several days. By that point I had started to give myself insulin injections every day, and I'd throw in a few extra shots when I'd start to feel sick. Since I was drinking every night, a lot of times I couldn't keep track; I'd pass out and be in pretty bad shape in terms of blood sugar by the time I woke up. I thought all I needed to do was be regular with my shots, but as I know now, it just doesn't work that way.

It really caught up to me in 2007, during the second season of *30 Rock.* That was the first time I ever took my health seriously. I came clean to the doctors about my drinking and how I'd been using the shots, and they were amazed that I was even alive. Once I understood what I'd been doing, I was amazed too. I wasn't malnourished in the traditional, Red Cross sense, but the way I was living, I was starving my body on the inside. During the last half of that season I got worse and worse, until my immune system broke down and I ended up with pneumonia. I had a high fever and I could hardly breathe. I finally went to the hospital, where my doctors found that the A1C level in my hemoglobin was 18 percent and had been for some time. A normal person's is typically between 4 and 6 percent; acceptable levels for a diabetic are between 6 and 8. My level was so high I should have been dead. I'll tell you how I managed to stay alive: adrenaline. It couldn't last forever, but like a soldier in battle, it kept me going during my touring years and especially once we started *30 Rock.*

Getting that sick was a sign from God that I had to get my

health together—and I listened. I'm just glad it wasn't too late. I also understood that I had to change my behavior. You're probably aware that I got into trouble for a few DUIs during those years. I did it right—I got fitted with an ankle bracelet and everything. They call it a SCRAM, which is pretty funny, because you ain't going nowhere with that thing on. My first DUI happened in Los Angeles in December 2005, and that incident got me strapped with probation. I went to this hot karaoke night with my boy Strong and got really fucked up because karaoke is just my thing. You've got to hear me, I'm telling you, I've got *soul*. I'm Jimmy Morgan's son—what do you expect? I do everything when I karaoke: throw on some Prince, Ray Charles, Michael Jackson— I'll kill you with my voice. So I had myself a good time until they closed—which, being L.A., was too damn early anyway—and I got ready to head home.

"Tray," my boy said, "let me drive you home."

"I got it, dude," I said. "I got it."

"I'm telling you, man, this is L.A. Let me drive you home."

"What you talkin' about, man? I know where I am."

"I'm telling you, dude, this is not New York. Don't fuck around. Let me drive you home."

"Nah, man, I got this."

I got into my Jaguar and got the fuck out of there, and as I drove home, the police started following me, probably right out of the parking lot. I wouldn't have known because I was enjoying my music and trying to keep the car on the road. When they pulled me over, they got me out of the car—I'm sure I smelled like a one-man club—and asked me to take a sobriety test.

"Please walk along the line, sir."

"Okay, Officer. I'm happy to."

I saw two lines, so I did what I thought was right: I walked both of them, one right after the other.

"Sir, what are you doing?"

"You ain't going to trick me! I'm walking both of these mother-fuckers. I know how you ask those trick questions."

"Sir, will you consent to a Breathalyzer test?"

"Hell yeah I will. I only had one beer like two hours ago."

They brought that thing over to me and I blew on it and sparks flew out the motherfucker. That's how drunk I was. They took me in, and when I got out I went right to the airport and got on the first plane out of there. By the time I was halfway across the country that shit was all over the news. Like I said, I ended up getting probation for that incident.

Probation didn't slow me down any, nor did it quiet my enthusiasm for either drinking or driving, which are two great appetites that don't go great together. I got back to New York and kept living out loud like I'd been doing. I definitely drove after having a few drinks, which was stupid, but I didn't have any problems again until November 2006, when I was arrested in New York for another DUI. That night I went to New York Giant Michael Strahan's birthday party. I was separated from Sabina by then, and I'd taken this Italian girl to the party with me, but she got on my nerves because she thought she was all that. So I barked on her at the party for acting that way, and she left. I'm convinced that she called the cops on me and told them that I was drinking and driving. I left there with my cousin and got on the West Side Highway, where they followed me from 27th Street all the way to 150th Street, where I was going to drop my boy off—and that's when they pulled me over. They weren't even in a cop car; they were in an undercover car disguised like a yellow cab. I wasn't even sure what was happening when they put those red and blue lights on behind me.

"What's this shit?" I said. "We got Starsky and Hutch behind us."

Once I realized the gravity of the situation, I hoped there was some way out of it, because another DUI when you're already on probation—that's a whole lot of trouble. Since the officers recognized me, I hoped that they were fans and that there was some way out.

"Officer, I'm going to be honest," I said to the guy. "I was drinking beer at a club, but I'm fine and I'm almost home. Can you give me a pass this time?"

"We can't do that, Mr. Morgan. Step out of the car, please."

By the time they got me to the precinct to book me it was already on TMZ.

I could have been sent to jail in L.A. for violating my probation in New York, but I was lucky enough to have a relatively clean record and a good lawyer. By the time we were through with all of the court appearances, I ended up pleading guilty to a DUI misdemeanor charge and agreed to undergo supervised treatment by a doctor and stay out of legal trouble for six months. I had to do community service too, and wear one of those alcohol-sniffing ankle bracelets.

But I wasn't going to let it bring my work schedule to a halt. I shot all of *First Sunday* with Ice Cube with that bracelet on, and went back to do most of the second season of *30 Rock* with it on too. As I said, this was the year that my health really hit rock bottom. One side effect of diabetes is that flesh wounds, like cuts and bruises, do not heal well. Cuts don't close up, and if they're not kept covered and treated right, they get infected and can become really dangerous. Diabetics have inefficient blood flow and an imbalance of the components that make up healthy blood, so something like a heavy bracelet on the ankle can do all kinds of damage, which it did to me. I started to develop a wound underneath it almost right away, and it got worse over time. My ankle swelled, and since the circulation was cut off by the bracelet, I could have developed gangrene in my foot—another hazard for diabetics. If the gangrene gets out of control, it can do so much damage that the foot may have to be amputated. This happens to diabetics more often than you'd think, and my ankle was definitely heading in that direction.

I tried to play it off as much as I could. I made jokes about the ankle bracelet, saying I was getting it blinged out by Jacob the Jeweler. And I made lots of public appearances during that time, at clubs, on Letterman and everything. It was a crazy thing to do because the way those bracelets work is that if you have alcohol vapors on your skin, a signal is sent to the police station and you get arrested. I'd be out at a club, not drinking, just hanging out, telling everyone in my booth to step off with their apple martinis so I wouldn't end up downtown. I was sitting on the couch one day, trying to put some ointment behind the bracelet to help protect my open wound. My son Tracy sat down and just stared at me like I was stupid.

"What's up, Tray?" I asked him.

"This is not cool, Dad," he said.

"You mean this cut I got back there? No, it's not."

"That's not what I mean, Dad. What if I start drinking and driving just like you? What happens if I get into an accident and get killed or kill some other people? What happens then? I'm going to be seventeen soon, you know."

That did it, right there, right then. Two DUIs and the threat of jail didn't do it and ten years of diabetes so bad that I might have lost my foot weren't enough either. But my son looking at me, disappointed, and drawing a very clear line between my lack of leadership as a parent and the effect it could have on him as a son got right through my thick skull. I cut drinking out of my life—first gradually, and then, after my health deteriorated later that year, altogether, forever. It really wasn't hard for me physically or mentally once I decided to do it. I didn't have to go to rehab because I never had a drinking problem in the first place. You might laugh when you read that, but it's true. Like I said, I knew it then and I know it now—I'm not addicted to alcohol. How can I say this? Because I *never* drank at home. I only drank socially. I'd go out and I'd want to get liquored up because everyone else was liquored up. That's the thing about me; I reflect whatever I see back at the world. If someone comes at me crooked, my reaction is to come back at him crooked. If I was in a room where everyone was drunk, I was going to get drunk too. When I was on *SNL,* I drank big every Saturday night because that was how we did it. Those after parties turned me into a social alcoholic, and I didn't even know it.

Sabina was great to hang in there and deal with most of my wild times, but those legal troubles pushed our relationship over the edge. I'd been misbehaving for too long, and that drinking shit on top of it would have been too much for anybody. Even Mother Teresa would have kicked my ass out of the house by then. I was always in the papers for doing crazy shit during those few bad years, and Sabina got real tired of hearing about it. She couldn't help me either because it was my trip to deal with—just like Martin had warned me—and I usually wasn't home under her watch when I was getting into trouble. She stood by me, but Sabina's no doormat. She eventually got fed up, and once a woman is fed up, there's nothing you can do to regain her love. If she hates you, that's fine, you've still got a chance. Fuck that; if she hates you, you're still *in*! But when she's fed up, it's over, because indifference is something else. Once that love turns, believe me, you're done. I know this from watching my mother and my

father. When a good woman's love goes cold, it never comes back.
That's when you've really got something to cry about.

You want to know the hardest part about finding love? When you get it, you want it to last so bad that you try to hold on to it even when you both know it's over. No one is to blame. It's the same reason you still root for a team that won the championship when you were a kid, even if since then they've sucked year after year after year. That's why New York still has Knicks fans, and why I'm one of them. I will always love the Knicks; I don't care if they don't see the playoffs again until 2026. When they do, I'll be courtside.

When we humans find something that makes us feel whole and connected, we don't want to let that shit go, no matter what it is. Even when everything is telling us we're wrong, even when everything in the relationship is pain, we hold out in the hope that we'll get that feeling back one more time. That's us, that's human. That's love.

Sabina and I got together in 1987 and we raised three kids. We were beyond best friends and lovers—we were each other's everything. It hadn't been bad all along; we hadn't been fooling ourselves. But things did start to go bad around 2003, and we separated in 2007. That break-up-and-make-up shit? We'd had four years of that. If you think about it, after twenty years together, that's the least we could do. So after being apart for a year, we tried it out again, but it didn't work. We finalized our split for good in 2008.

I'm gonna say something to all you people in relationships. Listen to me: If you feel like something is wrong, do not bother holding on—break up now. Don't expect anything to get better and don't expect people to change. If you're broken up, there's a reason for it and you should stay that way. If you get back together, there's a damn good chance it's just because you're having a hard time saying goodbye. If you don't have kids or some other reason to stay together, get out and move on with your lives.

I had to do it, but I sure as hell didn't want to. I had to give Sabina her life back. Like I said, it took us about four years to finally let each other go. At the time of this writing, we've only been apart officially for one year, unofficially for two. Up until the moment I signed those papers, I wasn't sure it was even going to happen. But that's love, and without it we humans are nothing.

All this talk about love and drama reminds me of someone from my past: Monique, my girlfriend for three years who lived out in Brooklyn when I was a kid. I was seventeen, and she was my first love, my puppy love. She was older than me, and she taught me things. Man, me and Mo . . . we had some times. Until she left me for an older guy whose fucking name I can't remember. That's enough about Mo. I mention her only because she truly broke my heart and taught me that nothing is forever. What did Mo get, a few lines in my book? Yeah, that's a few too many.

Looking back on this period, I wish I could fix some of the damage that was done to my relationship with my three sons. I wish I could have been home more, earning money locally so I would have been around for them. Before I got into show business, when my boys were little, I would take them to the park every day and do everything a dad should do. Once I got on the road I wasn't there every afternoon playing baseball or basketball with them like I used to, and they were old enough to realize I wasn't the dad they'd had when they were younger. I tried to make up for it when I got home, but that wasn't often enough.

Once I got busy, I got *busy*. I provided for them like never be-

fore and managed to keep them out of the kind of life I barely
survived, but I don't know if they'll ever understand it. To them
I'm sure it came down to this: *Our dad is not around.* I hope that
they know how much I love them and that the only reason I
wasn't around was because I had to provide. I'm sorry for all
those days I didn't spend with them. I can never get them back,
and no one besides my sons realizes that more than me. Maybe
someday soon or when they're a bit older we'll be able to talk
about it all and they'll see it differently than they do now. In the
meantime, I wish we were closer. It's harder now that I'm separated from their mother.

My wife and my sons were my whole world for my entire
adult life. That's why, even once I knew it was done between
Sabina and me, I still didn't really understand all that I was losing. I had let alcohol rule my life, and I paid the price: I nearly de-
stroyed my health and I drove my family away. I was the kind of
drunk who was a completely different man than he was when he
was sober.

Everyone knew it, and that guy I turned into had a name:
Chico Divine. Chico was a motherfucker who came out of the
depths of my mind and took over my body after about three
drinks. He was definitely my dark side, and he was 100 percent
hood. Chico was a wild card—you never knew what you were
gonna get when he came out, you just knew it was going to be a
party. It might be the kind of party where everyone cried and
Chico was the only one who had fun, but it was a party regardless. When Chico came out, somebody might get hurt and there
was a good chance someone's sister might get pregnant too. Chico
could be verbally abusive and was always loud and obnoxious,
but he was also wild, fun, and likeable—even lovable to some.
Chico was the kind of guy who had to take his shirt off when he
danced because he couldn't find the rhythm of the music trapped

in all them clothes. Chico was that crazy dude you see hanging from the rafters at the club on, like, Wednesday at six o'clock in the morning.

After a while, I realized it was either him or me, because there was no way the two of us could share one body peacefully. So I had to figure out what to do with Chico. He wouldn't move out, because he lived in here too, so I had to put that G to work for me. He could stay if he earned his keep, so I started to bring that Chico energy out onstage, and now he's my vehicle in the club. Now he drives me to and through my stand-up. But back then, he just drove me crazy. In my last few years at *Saturday Night Live,* Chico showed up every week at the after party. He definitely became the president of my fan club and my road manager during those years. When I went out on the road, Chico always did a late-night set, no matter what town we were in or what room we were in. And once we'd made it back to our hotel, Chico would usually stay around to work out new material even if I was the only one still awake! Chico would go out with at least thirty people, and he made sure that every single one of them got fucked up. One time Chico got so drunk he threw up in the club Suede in New York, right there in his booth—I think that one made Page Six. My boys had to carry me out. And I had to be on Wendy Williams's radio show four hours after that! The best or worst part of that story was that Chico threw up right on the foot of the lady who was the William Morris Agency's publicity director. There she was, this tall, well-dressed white lady, and Chico just threw up right on her shoes.

I somehow got through Wendy Williams's show, but it all got worse when I got home. I walked in my house and went right to the cat's litter box and took a shit and pissed all over the mother-fucker. My ex-wife woke up and found me there, still drunk, trying to squat in that thing so I didn't make a mess. She just shook her head. She was laughing, but she just shook her head. And it wasn't the last time I got caught like that! Man, that used to be a problem. I'd get drunk and the litter box would seem more appealing than the goddamned bathroom. Chico did all kinds of shit.

Then there was one night in 2004 when Chico ended up at Prince's house. It was the night before the Grammy Awards and my joke writer Bradley Lewis and I were going to Clive Davis's famous black-tie pre-Grammy party. We decided to start with some pregame partying at about five o'clock. We ended up running into Method Man, Redman, and the RZA, and we started going hard, drinking and smoking and having a good time. Sometime during that pre-party, Chico came out, and he decided to start calling Redman by his government name, Reggie Noble. All of a sudden, Red goes from getting high and having a good time to staring at me, all tense in the face. He stayed like that for about ten minutes as I dug myself out. All those nights I'd spent in front of tough audiences came in handy—I did whatever I could to soothe his aggression. I reminded him that he'd called himself Reggie Noble in one of his songs, and then I just gassed him up real good until we were boys again. I had to do that because Redman is one big dude and even Chico didn't want to get into it with him.

The next stop was Clive's party, but on the way we got pulled over by the cops because, to be honest, we should not have been driving. The cop was black, though, and somehow he just let us go. He recognized me and all that, but as I can tell you from experience, that does not mean shit. Man, where was that guy when I really needed him? Clive's party was held in a banquet room at the Beverly Hills Hotel and was all formal, with finely dressed people and well-appointed tables. We rolled in drunk as hell. I said hi to Robin Williams, who was sitting behind us. And then, during Fantasia's performance, I went to the bathroom, and in the hallway outside, Chaka Khan tried to tongue-kiss me. I'm serious—Chaka just leaned in and went for it, and her breath smelled like Bacardi and franks. My boys didn't believe me, so when she came back from the bathroom I pointed at her and said, "See! There she is! She just tried to kiss me!" After that I remember going over and saying hi to Jay-Z and Beyoncé and running into Stephen Belafonte, who is married to Mel B from the Spice Girls. Stephen told us about this party up at Prince's house, and he rolled with us up there.

We showed up at Prince's place in the Pacific Palisades and rolled through the front gate with the huge Prince symbol above it. The doors opened and there's Prince, in silver and red silk pajamas, no shoes, playing with his band on a stage by the pool. He's got his pool packed end to end with purple roses floating on top of the water—looked like a carpet of motherfucking roses over the motherfucker. Prince is jumping from instrument to instrument; he's got a full band, all of that. I ended up playing pool with Mekhi Phifer and a whole bunch of guys and everyone was having a great time. We're at a house party and a Prince concert at the same time! Can you think of anything better than that?

At one point I walked outside to find Damon Dash just destroying Paris Hilton, which I thought was really funny. Everyone stopped what they were doing and watched, because he was laying into her like I think so many people wanted to do right about then, in 2004. He was in her face, saying, "You don't do shit! What the fuck you *do*, anyway? What are you famous *for?*" He was crushing her, just grilling her in the head. Dame had just had enough of her being everywhere he looked, and for no good reason at all. Everybody had to love Dame right then for doing that. It was much deserved. She put her little dog in her purse and stormed the fuck out of there real quick.

This party went on all night—booze was flowing, liquor was good, and the music was off the meat rack! Before you know it, it's six-thirty or seven the next morning and everyone's gone. The only guests left are me, my boy Bradley, and these two girls we were talking to. We were sitting, chilling on a couch, just the four of us, and I looked up and Prince was standing there at the front door with his wife.

"Tracy, excuse me," he said. "You have to leave. The party is over."

He walked us to the door, and then I grabbed him by the back of his neck, pulled his face close to mine, looked him right in the eye, and said, "I have to tell you something, man. My father loved 'Condition of the Heart.' "

"Yeah, yeah, yeah," Prince said. "Motherfucker, get out."

"Thank you, man," I said.

Bradley and I were both lit, but we decided that he was going to drive us home. We had room for one more blunt before we took off. So we rolled one in Prince's driveway and left cigar residue and everything all over the ground. As the sun was coming up, we smoked some weed, sitting at the top of the Palisades, looking out. It was nice, man. It was life at the top. Then we went down the hill, took that left turn on the 405, and cruised all the way home with the workday traffic. And on the way we dropped Stephen Belafonte off because we'd found him sleeping in the front seat of our car! We left him off by the Four Seasons, holding a huge bottle of Grey Goose, just standing there in his suit, talking on the phone, by the curb.

Chico didn't let it end there, though. The next night he got me banned from the Viper Room. He got me banned everywhere in L.A. I even got banned from Barney's Beanery. That place is an old shithole where rockers and everyone else have done every-thing. The Who used to do heroin in there, and they were kicking *me* out for bad behavior? I decided to pick a fight with some-body while my boys were in the bathroom, and it got racial real quick. We were drinking pitchers of beer to try to feel better after the night before, because we were hurting. My boy left and I had some words with some dude and before I knew it I was sur-rounded by ten huge white dudes. So I did the only thing that made sense: I went up to the biggest one and said "Fuck you!" right in his face. They were calling me nigger and shit, and as I'm getting into this with them, I look at the IHOP across the street and I see these cardboard boxes moving toward us. I realized it was a homeless guy who'd been listening and decided to come over and back me up. He wasn't having this shit at all. This guy looked like Smokey from the PJ's, and he comes out of his boxes while the white dudes are screaming "You fucking nigger!" at me. The homeless dude comes over real quiet and says, "What did you fucking say?"

Then he just hits this white boy straight out, knocks him right down. And then the white guy's friends start chasing the guy, and real quick this scene becomes something out of *The Benny Hill Show.* They're chasing this homeless guy around the parking lot and he's running away from them, ducking between cars, evad-ing them for like ten minutes! It was ridiculous. At one point the homeless dude stopped and looked at them and did the Road Runner—"Meep Meep!" My boy and I were dying! We gave the guy some money for cracking that dickhead in the face for us. Good times, I tell you.

You can probably see why all my friends, my girlfriends, and my wife hated me when I was Chico Divine. And you can prob-ably guess that Chico didn't give a shit and came around anyway. Chico was like a cousin who knows you have money and only shows up around the holidays. If I was hot anywhere during those years, you could be sure Chico would show his face—and you never knew where he'd end up by dawn. He's seen the inside of a few sewers and the back rooms of many strip clubs—he's had all kinds of times. Chico led a life, people. He's done some crazy shit. He did not give a fuck about anything, and that's why I had to put him in his place. I had to bury him. And he didn't die easy. For a while there, I had to fight hard to keep him in the ground.

All of that drinking and nonsense is in the past for me now, I'm happy to report. Now I get to see the whole day, from 9 A.M. to 10 P.M. Getting Chico under control didn't mean losing my edge, it just made me better at my job. Even at my worst, when that mic goes on, I go to work. I forget everything except what I'm doing in that moment. That is the real rush—performance— not drinking or drugs. Richard Pryor taught me that. In his autobiography, written not too long before he died, he said he realized that none of the drugs were worth it, that he didn't have to do any of it to be funny. He finally realized, much too late, that he was naturally funny. Once you depend on a substance to make your funny, that's when you're really dead.

Doing stand-up for those years before *30 Rock* ruined my home life, but it also did something important for me. It brought me back to my roots. At *SNL* I had access to the mainstream, so I tried to market myself to everyone. I had the chance to expand my audience beyond black or white—I had the chance to reach everyone in America at once. That had never been an option for me before. By year seven, I had developed a cast of characters to play that got all kinds of people laughing.

But I'd lost sight of my roots. When I hit the road after my sitcom fell apart, I got back in touch with black stand-up. It was like coming home—I'd missed my people. Getting back on that circuit kept my spirits high and allowed me to develop into the comic I am today. I brought that universal appeal I'd developed at *SNL* back to the black comedy tradition that is at the heart of what I do. Bringing those two sides of myself together made me funnier than ever; it gave me the flavor that most of you reading this know me for.

I was also pushing my acting career whenever I could, and once I started to feel that change in my stand-up and in myself, I started to get called back for auditions. I appeared in *The Longest Yard* with Adam Sandler and Chris Rock, playing a prison cross-dresser and cheerleader, and I played Damon Wayans's sidekick, Percy, in *Little Man*. I did some voice work In *Are We There Yet?* and a few smaller roles here and there. But even if I had nothing but a few minutes and a few lines in anything, my goal was always the same: Steal the fucking scene. I didn't care who was in it with me, I was taking it home. It could have been all of my heroes, I still would have shot for the hoop without passing the ball.

At every audition, no matter what it's for, I give 150 percent. I've seen people go into auditions worried about who else is there and how they did, and all the worrying kills them before they even read for the part. I always walked into auditions like the part was already mine. Now people pitch movies to *me*. I've got a stack of them sitting right here, and I'll tell you something—you should see what I'm doing next.

That show and that whole world were born out of Eddie's *Delirious* and *Raw*. *Def Comedy Jam* took young black comics from the New York scene and put them on TV and allowed to be who they were. Suddenly there was a whole new possibility in black comedy. Eddie started it, and then *Def Comedy Jam* made it an institution. Comics wore what motherfuckers in hip-hop clubs were wearing. That show did for comedy what Run-DMC did for hip-hop: It allowed the whole world to hear the kinds of jokes we told—jokes about crackheads, jokes about weed, jokes about getting arrested by the cops. Word spread across the nation. Thanks to *Def Comedy Jam,* black comics no longer had to be generic.

Top of the Rock

There's one thing you've got to understand: I love Tina Fey so much, you people don't even know, man. I *love* her, I love her husband, Jeff, and I love their daughter, Alice. I love her like she is my own blood—no, I love her even more than that. She's my sister, Tina Fey. I'm convinced that we were brother and sister in a past life—I really feel that way—because Tina understands who I am as a person and what my strengths are as an actor and a comedian more than anyone I've ever met. I don't hide who I am, but at the same time, I'm not someone who explains myself—Tracy Morgan don't come with Cliffs Notes. Tina was a rare person in my life; she needed no explanation of who I was. She knew how to relate to me, and she got to know me on a personal level. She saw my untapped potential.

Tina and I had a connection from the first time we started talking about life and comedy, and it's done nothing but grow stronger all these years. Maybe it was because we were both underdogs at *Saturday Night Live*. She was coming up through the ranks as a young female writer, and I was the only black guy in the cast. Because Tina really seemed to know who I was, she understood how I could really shine in scripted comedy.

I still can't believe that I'm the first person she called when she started casting *30 Rock*. It's the truth: Tina called me before Alec Baldwin, before anyone. That means the world to me because at that time I had failed—my big network show got canceled without even getting through one season. It didn't matter to Tina. She handed me a second chance. It was like a dream come true when Tina called.

"I have a character for you, Tray," she said.

"You do?" I said. "What is it? Tell me."

"It's you. It's just you doing you."

As all of you who have read this far know by now, I've had a lot of people come along and help me in my career, and I'm thankful to them all and I'd never say anything to minimize what they did for me. But I have to give it up for Tina. She was the one who realized that you've got to let Tracy Morgan be fucking Tracy Morgan. That's because Tina knows who and what I am: I'm not evil, I'm not diabolical, I'm just a funny motherfucker. So she created a character that gave that to the world, a character who says, "Here is Tracy Morgan's beauty."

Television shows don't happen overnight, and *30 Rock* was no exception. Tina had the concept for the show two years before it became a reality, but the moment she pitched it to me, I was in. Then as things began to take shape I got even more excited. I ran into Alec Baldwin when he was hosting *Saturday Night Live*

around 2004, and he told me he was definitely going to do Tina's
show.

The genius of *30 Rock* is that from day one, Tina and the writers had every character clearly defined. From Jenna to Kenneth to Jack, every single character was fully 3-D and extremely well cast. From the moment I read that first script, I knew what Tracy Jordan was about: a famous black actor who endured some embarrassment and public scandals and who fell from grace a little bit. Tracy Jordan just went a little crazy, that's all. At that point in time, in the real world, we'd seen Dave Chappelle go through some madness and Martin go through his thing. I'm really cool with those guys, and I'm especially tight with Martin. I didn't want to offend him, so I was concerned about some of the aspects of being Tracy Jordan. People thought of Martin right away when they saw the character and when the media started writing about the show. Sure, there are similarities, but Tracy Jordan is not based on Martin because Martin didn't corner the market on buggin' out. Still, I felt bad when the media started to make Martin comparisons, but Tina set me straight. She reminded me that Martin publicly made fun of himself about the trouble he'd gotten in, so I shouldn't feel like I was mocking him or airing his dirty laundry. If you all haven't seen it, you should go buy his stand-up DVD *Runteldat*—he makes more fun of all the stuff he did than anybody else ever could.

Tracy Jordan is based on everybody that ever wigged out, myself included. To tell you the truth, my inspiration for Tracy Jordan doesn't come from any of those guys or even my own personality. People close to me have struggled with all kinds of mental instability. All the paranoia and delusion and imagination that you see in Tracy Jordan is my interpretation of them. They acted crazier on a regular basis than Dave, Martin, and I put together.

I guess that people relate to my character because the shit he's going through is the same shit they read about from my life in the headlines. Also, Tracy Jordan is more familiar to people than some of the other characters on the show. Look at it this way: How many people who watch *30 Rock* are friends with top network executives? Not many. How many are friends with female head writers of comedy shows? Not many. How many people know crazy black motherfuckers? A lot! I added multiple examples of bad behavior to Tracy Jordan's repertoire during Season 1 because at that point I was still partying like it was 1999. I was still ignoring my diabetes and hitting the clubs. Things were looking good professionally: I was on a show with an amazing cast and great writers, and it looked like we had a hit on our hands. That was enough for me to ignore my personal issues. I was so energized by the show that it carried me through. I was caught up in my madness at that point, still living out loud, drinking and putting on a Tracy Morgan show whenever I went out in public. Once the show started airing, once it was critically acclaimed, I rode an even greater high, which to me meant I had no reason to stop doing what I was doing.

My life on and off the camera became strangely similar there for a while. I was going out and partying all night, being crazy, and then showing up the next morning at Silvercup Studios in Queens to shoot *30 Rock* and portray a guy who acted crazy all the time. I was usually hungover but capable enough that it didn't affect my work.

Don't think for a minute that I was method acting, though. I didn't become Tracy Jordan, and Tracy Jordan isn't just Tracy Morgan with a different name. If you have any doubt about that, consider this: Our last, most successful season of the show, Season 3, I did entirely sober. I worked out as much as I could during that

season, and I ate right for the first time in my life. To me, that was
Tracy Jordan's best season; it was the one where he acted crazier
than ever and I think my performances were the best I've ever
done. And so does the Academy, people. I've just been nominated
for an Emmy for outstanding supporting actor in a comedy!

I don't have to be drinking and partying to play someone like
that—it's called *acting*. And now that I've got myself together, I
can really point at the divide between what I do and who I am.
Put it this way: Superman can't walk around all fucking day with
his cape and suit on. He's got to go back to being Clark Kent, a
mild-mannered motherfucker, sometimes. If he spent the day in
his cape and tights around the *Daily Planet,* he'd get paper clips
thrown at the back of his head. All of his co-workers would talk
about him around the water cooler. Superman needed two iden-
tities, and so do I—my personal life and my professional life.

I kept up that confusing charade pretty well during the first
season, but by the time we got around to the second season, it was
a whole different ball game. I really hit the wall and got very, very
sick with complications of my diabetes. It all came on the tail end
of my troubles with the law and the crumbling of my marriage.
By the end of our shooting schedule in spring 2007 I was in such
bad health that I would shoot at the studio all day and spend the
night in the hospital. I wasn't going to miss a day of work—and I
didn't—but my condition had gotten so out of control that after a
long day of shooting I needed comprehensive medical attention. I
would go straight from the set to a room in the hospital where I'd
be put on an IV to regulate my blood sugar. That's where I'd
spend the night, and the next day I'd go back and shoot my
scenes. It was the only way I could get through those last few
weeks. My condition was so bad that the doctors thought they'd
have to amputate my foot because of the infection from my court-

ordered ankle bracelet. My A1C level was 18 percent and had been for some time. My doctors told me over and over again that they had no idea how I was still living with a count like that. I had let a diet full of starch and liquor alter my blood chemistry for years, and as I said, I think the only reason I'm alive is that the adrenaline boost I get from entertaining saw me through.

One thing was for sure: I wasn't going to let my bad decisions ruin everything good that was going for me. I'd come too far to fuck up on *30 Rock,* even if it meant sleeping in a hospital bed with needles in my arms every night for three weeks. I wasn't going to let Tina down, I wasn't going to let the cast and crew down, and I wasn't going to let myself down either. So I did what I had to do.

One night when I was in that hospital room all alone, I re-solved to change. I couldn't allow this wake-up call to get by me, and I couldn't just rely on modern medicine to be my Band-Aid once again. For over ten years I'd looked at my health as just an-other hurdle that I needed to jump over when I came to a crisis, and I never looked back. I couldn't keep living like that. I wouldn't keep living like that. I finally realized that when it came to my health, I was still in ghetto survival mode: I took care of things only when I had to, and I never thought of the future be-cause I didn't expect to have one. That night, it all became clear to me: I should have been dead already. It was 3 A.M. and I was all alone in a dark room. I had a view from the window that looked out over the FDR Drive. I could almost see the Silvercup sign where we shoot the show. And I felt like I'd been hit by a truck—my body was sore, swollen, and retaining water where it shouldn't have been. My mind was spinning. I couldn't sleep and I couldn't quiet my head. I thought back on all I'd done in my life—the good, the bad, and everything that was going on in the now. I'd taken care of my wife and my children the best I could, and I was finally truly proud of what I was doing. And that's when I started to cry because I was afraid—afraid of losing my foot, afraid of losing my life, afraid I might not live long enough to enjoy the fruits of my labors. The tears started rolling down my cheeks and wouldn't stop. I just lay there, alone, being more honest with myself than I'd ever been. I stared out the window with the scenes of my life playing before my eyes.

My tears kept coming, but I felt them clearing my vision. I finally began to see things as they were and knew that I had to change right away, no excuses. There was only one way to enjoy everything I'd struggled so hard to have—and that was to live a happy and healthy life. Not to limp through life the way I'd been doing for years, but to do whatever it took to walk tall, proud, and strong. If I lost my foot because of my own ignorance, I wouldn't be able to look myself in the mirror. If I lived less than the best life I could live, I would be a failure. If I died before my time and let my kids grow up without a father, I would be a failure. I would leave them no better off than I'd been, and to my mind every generation is supposed to do *better*. I could not get that simple idea out of my head—I had to do *better*. I tried not to worry too much about how and why I'd gotten lost; through my tears I told myself to concentrate only on how quickly I was going to be found.

Thank God I had Taneisha in my life; she is my angel and my heart and my blessing from God. When she came into my world, all the drinking and the bad eating stopped and all the working out and being healthy began. She was my inspiration because she leads by *example*. I had resisted here and there because I don't like being told what to do any more than the next man, but that night in the hospital I decided to put my health in her hands and embrace that change with everything I had. That night I thought about all the beautiful things I had lost and all that I had neglected because I got caught up being this Tracy Morgan mother-fucker. I didn't even know who that guy was anymore—I just knew who he *wasn't.*

That night I realized something else: I couldn't blame Sabina for leaving me. She got tired of the roller-coaster, and I don't blame her. I was in the newspaper for embarrassing shit all the time—it was *years* of that—until she finally said, "I've got to move on, I've got to go. You're not growing up." There was no other road for me, though, because after my father died I was given no guidance. I had no one to turn to and very few people aside from friends like Martin to talk to about the kinds of pressure I was going through. I was too proud anyway, and I didn't like to rely on anybody. There was only one way for Tracy Morgan to learn his lessons, and that was the hard way. I had to earn my maturity the same way I had to earn my success. It didn't happen soon enough, but thank God I saw the writing on the wall in time. I could have lost it all, but I turned it around and grew up. I feel like I've just come into my manhood in the past three or four years. That dark night in the hospital was like making that last turn on the track before the home stretch in a race: It took me where I needed to be.

What I was doing in my personal life was also burning me in my professional life because I hadn't learned to take that fucking Superman suit off. I wore that shit to bed, I wore it to work, and I never sent it to the cleaners. That was all fine and good when I was out there doing my own thing, but when I got into legal trouble during the first and second seasons of *30 Rock,* I felt terrible because on top of it all, I was letting Tina Fey down. Who was to blame? No one but me, myself, and I. Let's face it, there are a lot of funny black comics out there; Tina could have gotten anybody to play Tracy Jordan. But she put her faith in me and relied on me to make that character what he is. The last thing I wanted to do was repay her by bringing negative publicity to the show or jeopardize the shooting schedule in any way.

That is why I never had a problem with the writers taking anything from my personal life and using it for plotlines. I don't live with regret—I use my mistakes every way I can. We call that "having your dues up." It was something we did at *SNL*. You expose your flaws so the writers have something to inspire them and you have material you can really identify with. When I was in the headlines and wearing ankle bracelets, Tina never had to ask me if it was okay to use all that for the show. She already knew it was okay—I gave all of that to them because it was common knowledge. It's different for me than for some of the other members of the cast. I'm a comedian—everything in my life is material. I turn tragedy into funny for a living, and our writers know that. Think of Alec Baldwin's situation with his daughter, for example. They could have made fun of that, but I'm not so sure Alec would have gone for it. He might be the lead actor in a TV sitcom, but Alec Baldwin is one of the greatest dramatic actors of our time. He's definitely not a comedian. His personal life is not the source material he turns to for laughs; it belongs to him and exists outside of his career.

Me, I'm another story. The writers couldn't write a Tracy Morgan character on their own because the shit in my life is so twisted it *has* to be real. You don't need to be Sherlock Holmes to figure out that most of the shit on the show came from my fucking headlines. Tina knows Sabina; she knows my kids. My kids were raised around *Saturday Night Live,* and Sabina was around the studio all the years I was there. Tina knew all of the drama we went through in our relationship. Shit, she even knew that I keep exotic pets like piranhas, snakes, and lizards. It made sense to use all of that as material to create Tracy Jordan. Why waste it? I wouldn't have it any other way. Listen, my idol is Richard Pryor, and if there's one thing I learned from him, it's that your entire life should be up for grabs. Anything you do or live through should be fodder for your comedy. He documented everything in his life through his characters and his stand-up. He had no shame and no pride about it—even when he lit himself on fire trying to freebase cocaine and nearly died, he made a hilarious routine out of it. Because that is what true comics do.

Of all of the episodes that came from my personal life, one of the funniest ones for me is the one in which Tracy Jordan is convinced that his sons want to kill him. I think all children of celebrities, or even kids whose parents have very demanding jobs, feel neglected at times and want to get at their parents for that. If you're a parent who is away from home a lot, there will come a point when your kids will be angry at you for it, and in some way they're going to let you know. The way it played out on the show was entirely the product of the writers' imaginations because my kids never wanted to kill me. My kids love me. But in that episode Tracy is convinced that his boys are going to "Menendez" him, when all they're trying to do is get his attention and spend some time with him. I can relate to that because my kids are teenagers now and they're definitely at that point where they're acting up. They're getting attention from girls at school, they're playing football, and they think they can take the old man. I went through it, we all go through it. Just like Will Smith once rapped, "Parents just don't understand." The Tracy Jordan version of that, of course, is that they're going to kill him.

Thanks to my work on *30 Rock*, I've learned about timing, I've learned about chemistry, and I've learned how to play off of my cast mates more than I have on any other project I've ever done. The funny is my gift—that just don't get better—but through doing table reads and running lines as much as we do on the show, I've polished my abilities, and I think it shows.

The schedule on the show would make a professional out of anyone because it is very rigorous. *Saturday Night Live* was one thing—it was tiring and there was always the uncertainty of whether or not your skits were going to see airtime. But there was a rhythm to it that you got used to after a while. *30 Rock* is completely different. If *SNL* is like running a one-hundred-yard dash, *30 Rock* is more like cross-country—it's a longer and more irregular course. It's up to you to pace yourself and find the inner reserves to carry you through.

Usually we shoot two episodes a week. We work at Silvercup Studios, which has several soundstages, so we'll have two sets going at once on two adjoining stages, with two completely different camera crews, usually shooting two entirely different shows. And at some point during that week—we never know exactly when—we'll have a table read for the next episode. There's no live taping and no studio audience to perform for, so we keep our own schedule. And the following week we do two more episodes. That's how it goes, five days a week, fifteen to eighteen hours a day, for about six months of the year. It's not for the faint of heart. And with the caliber of talent we have, every actor—no matter if you're a regular or you just have a cameo—has to bring her A game.

Our cast is great and we have a lot of fun, but we all have our own space and do our own thing. I don't hang out in Tina Fey's dressing room, and she doesn't hang out in mine. We're all professionals and adults. People think that we hang out all day long just being funny, like we're in college. I'm sorry to burst that bubble. We spend most of our waking hours on the set five days a week. No matter how much you like someone you work with, after working those kinds of hours, you've seen enough of them.

I don't bother Alec between scenes—the man doesn't want me in his dressing room making jokes all day long. TV is hard fucking work! It's long hours and many days away from your family. So we love each other and we do enjoy what we do, but when we're working, we're working. You don't get to the top by bullshitting around.

Obviously we're not bullshitting at all, because you don't sweep the prime-time Emmys like we did in 2008 without trying. At this point I can't even count how many nominations we've gotten since our first season. And this year, 2009, we've just racked up another twenty-two! The best thing about all of these awards we've won isn't the bragging rights, it's that every time we win something else, the network puts a bigger TV in my dressing room. I've now got a sixty-four-inch LCD in there, which means that Mitsubishi had better invent something new because we don't plan on losing awards anytime soon. The TV is nice, but what I really want is another zero at the end of my check. My producers know that because I remind them all the time.

I think they're going to have to honor that request after that speech I made on behalf of the show at the Golden Globe Awards in January 2009. Tina and I put that speech together, and I'd say it came off pretty well, wouldn't you? That is where the title of this book came from, because I laid it out. I said that we had a black president and that I was the voice of postracial America—which I am! That was the room to be in that night: Ron Howard was there clapping and laughing. I saw Clint Eastwood off to the side smiling like Dirty Harry just before he shoots another punk. That room was full of powerful people who probably didn't even know I existed until *30 Rock* won the award and I got up there. The moon and the stars had really lined up—Obama won, we won, it was perfect. There was just no way I couldn't mention Obama.

No one had mentioned him in their speeches all night long—I
couldn't believe that! I guess it took a young black motherfucker
from the Bronx and Brooklyn to come out and say some fly shit
like that to make everybody take notice. For a minute I wondered
if it was the right thing to do. Must have been, because fuck it,
now I'm making movies.

In the first three seasons of *30 Rock* I had some great times
amidst some hard times. I have memories I'll never forget and
scars that have healed but won't go away. One of the best times
took place in 2007, on my birthday. We were shooting an episode
in which Gladys Knight had a cameo. During one of the breaks I
was called out of my dressing room, and there was the cast and
crew, and there was Gladys Knight singing me "Happy Birthday." That was *Gladys Knight,* dude! Singing to me, a kid from
the ghetto. I'll never forget that. I'll also never forget having
Salma Hayek on set last season. That was incredible and almost
distracting. If I had to choose one, I'd say she is my favorite guest
star ever. I asked Tina if we could have a subplot where Salma
has a very explicit pornographic affair with Tracy Jordan. She
didn't go for it, but I'm hoping we can revisit that idea in the future. I'm telling you, whenever Salma came around, it was just
me and her. She is my *baby.* If she gave me just a little time, I
would make her the Octomom.

The last thing I want to say is that there's one simple reason
why *30 Rock* is so important to me. It's because we're number one
and I've never been number one at anything. When I was born, I
was number two. When I met my wife, she already had two kids,
so I could never be number one in her life. During Season 3 of the
show, my relationship with Taneisha became deeper and that's
when I became number one to her. She makes me feel like that
every day. She tells me all the time, "I've got brothers that I love,
I've got nephews that I love, but you're number one to me." Well,

actually, to Taneisha, God is number one, but behind Him I'm second to none.

As far as my professional life goes, *30 Rock* is number one to me. I've never had a number one movie at the box office, but being on the top show of 2008 and 2009, that's everything to me. Anyone who wants the belt has got to come get it from us. It's everything I've worked so hard for in this business. And now I'm enjoying it with a clear head. *All in the Family, Seinfeld, Good Times, Martin, The Cosby Show*—they were all number one. And now it's our turn.

BLACK COMEDY IS
The Nineties Marriage of Hip-Hop and Comedy

When hip-hop and comedy met on shows like *Def Comedy Jam*, *Uptown Comedy Club*, and more, a whole lot of talent emerged: Chris Tucker, Martin Lawrence, Cedric the Entertainer, Steve Harvey, Bernie Mac, and me, Tracy Morgan. Bernie Mac worked as a comic for years, waiting for this moment to happen. And once it did, all of us got on. This movement was born in the nineties and made stars out of us. Pat yourselves on the back, motherfuckers, because we made it happen.

CHAPTER 7

I'm a Full-Grown Man

There's one thing people have to understand: Comics are not happy clowns. They are dark people, all of them, no matter how they grew up or what color they are. Anyone who has devoted his life to comedy and making people laugh wants to see that joy reflected back at him by rooms full of people because he's never seen that kind of happiness anywhere else. Comedians are comedians because they *need* that laughter and joy; it fills a hole in them. Some of them will never get that hole filled either. For some comics, no amount of success and no amount of laughter is enough—that pain can never be relieved, that emptiness can never be satisfied.

You know what you'll find in a lot of comedians' darkness? Anger. Lots and lots of anger. And we're not the only performers that entertain you out of anger either. Michael Jackson danced out of anger. He didn't have a good home life; he was ordered around by his dad and made to work like a slave. I'm no slave, but otherwise I'm no different from Michael Jackson when I'm onstage: When I'm out there I am fucking *angry*. I talk about the shit in life that pisses me off. When is the last time you heard a comedian take the stage and talk about the happy parts of his marriage? Never! All you hear comedians talk about is the fucked-up shit. I'll tell you why that is—because it's funnier!

As someone who has spent time on the stage and in the audience, I can tell you from both sides of the coin that when a comedian makes an honest connection with an audience, something happens to the room. If you're onstage talking about your life and people in your audience have similar issues and can relate, you establish *contact*. That was something I was told to look for and try to do back in the workshop all those years ago at the Uptown Comedy Club. If you establish contact, you've built a bridge from your act to your audience through your story—it's like you've called them on the phone and now you're talking. You've managed to relate to them by sharing your story and allowed them to relate to you—and you've got them laughing their asses off. It's the best thing you can do to keep them engaged in your act. Instead of having them laugh *at* you, which they'd do if you just got up there and blew farts for thirty minutes, they are laughing *with* you. They hear your story and say, "Yo! I am going through the same shit! That guy up there is just like me."

When I first started out doing stand-up, I thought I had to take people to some crazy place to make them laugh. I thought I had to impress them with my imagination, to take them on a wild ride to a made-up world, and once we were all there together, I could tell them about myself and my life through the cast of characters I'd created. That worked for me as a younger, less experienced comic, but as I got older and wiser, I realized that reality contains the most powerful material of all. Sure, I can make up a guy who represents something I think or something I've been through, but I'm much funnier without that mask. When my audience hears a story and I'm right there, as me, acting it out and telling every detail, that's powerful. That's bigger funny because that's me bringing the honesty. My comedy today isn't based on a figment of my imagination—it's all real. It's like a giant turkey that I cook onstage, keeping it nice and moist by basting it in reality.

That turkey is my heart and soul, and I've got to protect it. When you're young, you take your skills for granted because you think you're Superman. But experience teaches you that you have to look after the things you value. I value the gift of comedy that God gave me. That don't mean I keep it in a vault, it just means that now I treat it right. I take it out and romance it, I get its oil changed, you know what I'm saying? I *nurture* my funny—I tell it bedtime stories, I send it flowers and buy it presents—because I'd be dead without it. Even if I wasn't a comedian, I'd need it just to get through life. If I wasn't able to make people around me laugh and if I wasn't able to laugh at my own life, I'd have been dead a long time ago.

When Sabina and I were splitting up, nobody knew how hard it was on me. I was a professional; I wasn't going to let anyone know that my world was falling apart. When I got onstage or in front of the camera, I did what I had to do—I took my pain and used it however I could. It wasn't as easy to be funny, it took more effort and more energy, but I threw myself into it. I asked God to help me, and He saw me through. My faith is strong. God did not bring me this far to see me fall—I truly believe that. All the loved ones I've lost in the game and in life—my father, my grandmother, my uncles, and my boys Allen and Spoon—they are all looking out for me. I feel their presence around me all the time, more and more every day.

I don't think I'm on a mission from God or that I've been chosen—nothing like that—but my faith in God has been repaid. But faith alone isn't enough. You can't just have faith and wait— you've got to prove your faith and prove you're worthy. I almost died because of my negligence, but I'm not going to make those mistakes again; I'm going to keep my faith strong and pay it respect. I know now when I get onstage that no matter what happens, even if thirty thousand people boo me, I will *live.* And life cannot be taken for granted.

God's mercy is why I'm here today. You've read this far, so you're probably wondering how I could feel that way with all of the hard times I've seen. My father had the same faith. Surviving Vietnam? That had to be a work of God. The odds were against him living through that, especially with his addiction blurring his mind and eating away at his strength. A soldier on heroin is *vulnerable.* That soldier is an easy target because he's walking wounded. The only way my father got home was God.

One of my father's greatest accomplishments was dying at peace. When he died much too young, at age forty, he wasn't angry. He was angry when he first learned he'd contracted AIDS from sharing needles, but he used his faith to work through that anger. He grew weak, his body began to give out, and in no time he became a shadow of himself. But as he wasted away physically, he grew larger spiritually. His faith never wavered, straight up to the end, long after a lot of good men would have been cursing God and pitying themselves. When it was his time to go, he was truly at peace. I used to have anxiety that I was going to be a failure. Now that I'm his age and I'm healthy, that weight is off me. My father never got to meet his grandkids; that's the next step for me.

My father saw it like this: The Lord knew what he'd done in Vietnam and was making him pay the price. My father thought it was his bill to pay. He'd killed men, like every soldier does to survive at war. But that's not what my father was talking about. To him, choosing the dope was his failure. He was weak, he'd shot dope into his arms, and the dope took him over. He lost his judgment, he shared needles, and once he was out of the jungle and off the dope, happy with his life, it was time to pay the price— *with his life.*

But like I said, he was at peace with it by the end. He didn't blame it on the war or the government; he laid it on himself, and his faith helped him find a way to forgive himself. That is what it means to be a man. He couldn't have taught me that lesson any other way. In the years I had with him, he taught me many things by the way he lived, but he could have only taught me this lesson by the way he died. It was hard for me when my dad first got sick, because I was a pigheaded teenager who was still mad that he'd left me the first time. Once I knew I was going to lose him again, I was angrier than ever because this time was forever. I blamed him for it, and I also hated that he had AIDS because of what people would say when they found out. It made our last few months together definitely not what they should have been. I stayed away from him for a while, and I was full of anger when I saw him. But as he got sicker, I realized that I was pushing him away and I tried to change that. I tried to talk to him and see him and spend as much time as I could with him. During one of the long talks we had in the hospital, he said to me, "Tray, I'm at peace." And I'm glad he told me that. It didn't make losing him easier, but it makes it easier looking back on his passing now.

I miss him every day, but I know he's with me. He's in this room with me as I write these words. And when I'm onstage, I know he's right there next to me, laughing sometimes. I'm completely serious. I've felt him there more than a few times. It makes me happy when I get that sensation because I want him right beside me, enjoying the same view. And no matter how raunchy I get, I know he's not leaving because Jimmy Morgan always spoke the truth. He hears all those words I use in my act that disgust some people and send them out the door early—I see you, brand-new white, blond, blue-eyed *30 Rock* fans! My dad knows the truth about those words: They come from the same place as the beautiful words, because everything in this world is connected. God gave me those words, so I've got no shame. I don't care what people say. If they can't take it, they should get out of the fucking room and let the rest of us communicate. When I'm onstage, I'm talking about what I know, not what you think I know or what you want to hear. Anybody can be Ray Romano, anybody can be Seinfeld. It's easy to find the middle of the road when the highway is eight lanes wide. I didn't grow up on that shit; I grew up on Richard Pryor, Redd Foxx, and fucking Eddie Murphy. That's where I'm from, that's how I am, and that's how it is. I got to keep it gully.

I've changed a lot in the last few years, and I'm not just talking about breaking out with *30 Rock* and landing roles in movies that I'd never have gotten five years ago. I'm talking about looking back on my entire life for the first time. Now that I know I've climbed a mountain, I'm taking in the view before I hike up the next peak.

It's like I'm in the box seats at the Tracy Morgan Theater watching the Muppets on Ice doing the story of my life for my birthday. Yo, Gonzo, holla at me! I'm up here! This point in my life is like the end of the second act. It's not the end, because I'm far from over. If my life was the *Star Wars* trilogy, which is really a sixilogy, we'd just be getting going. Right now the Ewoks would be dancing.

I'm experiencing a rebirth. Being born is painful—even when you do it again! You get this new life that you don't know what to do with. When my wife and I split, it was painful. That relationship was all I knew of trust. When I was on the road, when I was drinking, when I was having my legal troubles, those were dark days. None of my family reached out to me. It didn't take much to see that I was in trouble—all they had to do was read the closest newspaper. Fuck that, all they had to do was open a window, because when someone like me, a guy from the neighborhood who is on TV, gets popped for a DUI, every single motherfucker on the block is gonna be talking about it. Trust me, my family knew what was happening with me.

There was a lot of darkness. My wife wasn't around, my family didn't support me, I was always traveling to pay the bills, and I drank to drown my pain. Suicide and crazy thoughts come when people feel truly alone. That's when the devil gets in your head and fills you with doubt.

Either I was going to let loneliness drown me, or I was gonna learn to swim on my own. It wasn't like the clouds parted and light shone down on my face through my dirty hotel window one morning and a vision from heaven told me I would be fine. What happened was much more down-to-earth: I felt terrible and alone for weeks on end. I was also at a real physical low point, suffering from my own neglect. And when you are in that kind of a state, you do get to a point where you have an internal dialogue; you ask yourself if you're going to give up or go on. I'm a survivor, so there was only one answer for me, but I had to hear it inside before I could start pulling myself together. Somewhere during those dark days, I realized something that I had never considered before: It was *okay to be alone*. Maybe it was because I

was finally letting go of what I knew was already gone—
Sabina—or letting go of some other idea of what my life was supposed to be. Whatever it was, I knew I had God with me, so I was
never going to be totally alone. But other than Him, all I needed
was me.

I learned what everyone needs to know: Some solitude is good
for you, no matter who you are. Before a show, I need solitude to
get my head right because I've got to clear my mind and focus.
The bigger you get, the harder it is to find some quiet because
people don't want to give you space. There's a long line of people
who want some of your time, and they will take every last minute
you have to give if you let them. You know what? Looking back,
I'd like to think that's what my family was doing during my hard
times—giving me my space. They never said that's what they
were doing, but I'm going to choose to believe they were giving
me room to grow. I'd like to thank them for that because grow I
did. It's all good now.

I've got a new relationship in my life these days, which is something I wasn't looking for and didn't count on happening
again. In the movie *A Bronx Tale,* the narrator says that you get
one, maybe two good ones in your life. Well, she is my second
good one, that Taneisha. It took a lot of understanding to see me
through my split from my family. She was right there when she
didn't have to be, and that's what I love about her. She's younger
than me but she's wise; she knew I had to heal on my own terms,
and that meant I needed time and space. She's a strong woman, so
she was able to give me that.

Still, I tested Taneisha. How could I not? People say a lonely
man is the most bitter man you'll meet. That's bullshit—the
most bitter man in the world is a man who's getting divorced.

Bitter as a fucking lemon. Early in our relationship, I would take Taneisha to functions and put her in the room with some bigwig motherfuckers—folks way more high-profile, way more rich, and way further up the food chain than me. I'd make the rounds and keep an eye on her to see what she'd do. The girl never got distracted. She kept her eyes on me and never wavered. That's when I knew it was good: when I'd look in her eyes and see no one else but me. After she passed a few tests I could finally say to myself, "Okay, she's good. She's the truth. She's the real deal." It was only then that I could begin to open up my heart a little bit.

I'm telling you, I was hard to deal with, which some people might find crazy, because she's hot as hell too! And this is a *recession*! Which means that I'd better not push her away, because the minute things get better out there, she might fly the coop for some banker whose portfolio just rebounded. Don't matter to me at all—hot is only on the outside and looks don't last forever. I do not believe in finding a good woman anymore; I believe you've got to mold one to your liking. It's up to you to let a woman know that you don't like olives in your salad, and it's up to her to remember that.

Seriously, what Taneisha and I have is real; I know it in my heart. Even if I lost everything, I believe she'd stay with me. She wouldn't blame me for it, she wouldn't give a fuck. That's what I love about her. I can always make her laugh—even if she's crying. I hope I'll never make her cry, but I can't change the one thing that comes with being with me: Falling in love with a professional entertainer is inviting pain and heartache to your fucking front doorstep.

If you're with an entertainer, you have to share him with his public. Taneisha has learned that she's got to let me be with my public. I've seen how other women handle their men being approached by fans, and I can tell you, my lady is a gracious, graceful swan. Female fans often ask to have their picture taken with me. They move in for a hug and say, "Your girl ain't gonna get mad?" I've watched friends of mine go from signing autographs to breaking up fights. Their girls will be like, "Don't you be hugging my man in no picture, bitch! You can't take no picture with him." Taneisha has never done that. She never gets mad, because she knows she's got me. Nothing to get mad at if you ain't insecure. Taneisha is pure grace, just like a deer. When she smiles she lights up the room and makes my day better. I keep telling her that when we have a baby girl, we are going to name her Grace.

Taneisha also knows she has to let me run the street sometimes with my boys because that is where I get my information. I've got to stay connected to the real world and keep my ear to the ground if I'm going to stay real in my comedy. I can't write comedy bits up in my luxury apartment—that's where I live now, but that's not where I'm *from*.

My love affair with comedy is strong. Taneisha understands something very important: *That* love affair ain't going nowhere. She can get into bed with me and comedy and have a three-way because that's the way it is. She's a good girl—she didn't think she'd like that kinky shit until she tried it. I invite her into bed with me and comedy all the time, and most of the time she consents. She's laughing at me saying this right now, so me and comedy are going to get her in bed once again! We *bad,* comedy and me.

One of the many pieces of wisdom my dad impressed upon me is from the Bible, and too many people forget it: This too shall pass. All the good, all the bad, all of this earth around us— it all passes in time. If you get a slice on your arm, it will hurt that day and it will hurt the next day too. That cut will bleed. But in a month it will be nothing but a scar. Some of us get through life with small scars and some of us end up with Christmas trees on our backs, just like Denzel in *Glory.*

I'm a survivor. That's the legacy of the ghetto: If you get out, nothing else in the world can take you down except your own bad decisions. I can deal with whatever comes, whatever life throws at me, because I've already walked through worse. This is why I feel sorry for suckers like Paris Hilton. That bitch wouldn't know what to do if she had to work for a living or face some real struggle. She's got everything, and she's still bored. What is her career? She's got no talent—I've seen that porn video. She used her money to force her way into being famous, and when she got what she bought, it was suddenly a big problem for her. I feel sorry for her because she's just pathetic.

I've made mistakes in my life that had nothing to do with God or the devil. They were all me. I take all of the blame for the stupid shit I've done, just like I take the credit for removing all of the negative shit from my life. I'm through with people who drain my soul and my bank account, and I'm only devoting my love and energy to my children and to people who prove that they care about me. Back when I was in my party mode and everything was coming apart, I made a list of everything going on in my life. The good was on one side and the bad was on the other—and the bad list was a lot longer. It took me a few years to cut that side down because bad things don't die easy. But today that list is short. Once I dropped that drinking lifestyle, everything changed quick, because all of the negative people around me dropped off quick too. And I don't miss nobody.

Today I'm just maintaining, holding my head up and enjoying life. I'm not worried about the things I can't control. I'm staying natural and looking out for trickinology. Trickinology is when those closest to you play the fucking game in which they try to take from you and take you down. It's a mental game and you've got to be ready for it.

I was lost, but now I'm found. And I'm *riding*. I'm wandering too, learning what I can, just like I did when I was a kid. One of my greatest memories was the day I got lost at the Bronx Zoo when I was nine years old. I saw all of the animals I wanted, just going from one cage to another. I was so caught up that it took me hours to realize I was lost; I had wandered away from my family. That's what happens when I'm following my mind wherever it will take me—I end up in places I didn't expect to go.

I still like to wander because it's the best way to learn about the world. You'll be surprised what you'll find! I'll go explore parts of New York City and find them as segregated as the zoo. You don't see white people getting lost on purpose in the Bronx, just like you don't see black people doing that in Bensonhurst. It's too bad that motherfuckers here are so colonized, man, but that's the way it is. If you want to find black people, go to Brooklyn. If you're looking for Jamaicans, go to Flatbush. If you're looking for Do-minicans, go to Washington Heights. Head to the South Bronx to meet Puerto Ricans, and go to Riverdale to hang with Jewish peo-ple. Personally I don't pay attention to boundaries. I go wherever the fuck I want to go and I hang out with whomever I like. I don't care what color you are—if you're a good brother or sister, you're cool with me. I know some straight, solid white people who've done right by me just like I know some black people who are devils. My father taught me to see what was on the inside.

A reporter recently asked me what I'd do if I was given the superpower of invisibility. I told him, "I already have that super-power. I'm black." That is how black motherfuckers feel—invisible. White people don't see black people in America unless they have to. I was used to that, but now that I've got all of these white people recognizing me, saying they love me, *black* people

have been giving me looks like I'm letting *them* down. I look at
my fans' *hearts,* not their color. But if I judge you, I'm going to
judge you righteously. If you are not right, then you are not
right. How are you going to win when you ain't right within? I
understand why some of my black brothers and sisters feel that
way. Yeah, okay, there's not a lot of black people on NBC, but
I'm trying to reach a broader audience and no one should be
mad about that. There's no better way to do that than by being
one of the stars of the best sitcom on television, in a prime-time
slot, on a major network. Of course, I'm open to suggestions if
any of you have them. Holler them out when you see me on the
street walking my dogs, y'all. I'm serious.

One thing about me: I may be out of the ghetto, but I'm always
going to have my black rage. That's me and that's my edge. At the
same time, that rage is why I can't hang out in the hood no more.
The truth is that I'm not much different from everyone else in the
hood. All I had was one great idea—comedy—and that's why I'm
here. I worked hard and I'm happy to say it paid off.

My dad gave me the middle name Amado. As in "A'm a do"
for me, all right? You do you, and Amado me. I have the words
ME, MYSELF & I tattooed on my back. I do not feel peer pressure. I
turned forty last year. When I feel like leaving a club, I leave.
When I feel like getting in my car, I do that. I do like my man
Jay-Z says: "I need the freedom to say whatever I like, to write
whatever I like." There it is, simple and plain—I'm a full-grown
man.

I don't understand the squeaky-clean shit in comedy. To me,
you're not funny unless you can say *motherfucker* three different ways—
and *mean* it. It's a verb, it's a noun, it's a predicate nominative. If I ever do
Inside the Actors Studio and James Lipton asks me my favorite word? It's
motherfucker. I don't care who you are, everybody got to learn to say
motherfucker. Obama gonna say it one of these days. I don't know who
is gonna make him do it—might be North Korea, might be China, but
somebody is gonna piss him off and he'll be sitting there thinking about it
in his little black dress socks and he's just gonna turn around and say,
"Mother*fucker*! Goddamn it, Michelle, where is that fucking nuke button at?"
I think it's gonna be either North Korea or his mother-in-law.

I'm Tracy Morgan. Thank You for Being Here with Me Tonight! Now Please Go Home.

What else can I say about myself before you and I go our separate ways? Let me see. Every day I thank God for what I have because I'm lucky to be alive. That is a simple habit that I've gotten into lately, something I should have started doing years ago. I thank God for my gift of funny, because every time I check I've got big bags of it that I haven't even opened yet. I'm at an age where I'm mature enough to reflect on where I've been and to realize that I've come very far, against all odds. By forty, my father had raised his children, survived a war, and beaten a heroin addiction, but he was dying of AIDS. My son Tracy junior is the same age I was when my father died, and I am the same age that my father was when he passed away. I think about that all the time. You never know what life is going to hand you, so you've got to live right.

I'm doing the best I can as a father, and I hope that's good enough. I lost my father in 1987, and I wish I'd had him around to ask him, man to man, a few things about raising a child. Now that I'm an adult, I would have liked to have heard his perspective. My dad did say one thing to me that's always made sense: Life don't come with instructions. As a teenager I heard him but I didn't listen. Now I know how right he was.

I've learned to expect good things and to reflect on the positivity in my life, but to tell you the truth, sometimes I'm still surprised when things go well for me. I'm getting used to it, but I've had to overcome years of things going wrong and every day offering nothing but another set of mountains to climb. When you expect struggle every day, it's a little bit strange when you have smooth sailing for a change. Being part of an award-winning show is more than I ever dreamed of; it still feels like Christmas to me every time we take home another trophy.

One thing that comes with success is the money to spend on your lifestyle. I've always liked exotic pets, and now I can afford to fill my luxury apartment with them. I've got a thirty-thousand-dollar jellyfish tank, tarantulas, bird-eating spiders, eels, snakes, dogs, piranha, and sharks. I'm like Michael Jackson! I once asked my wife why she thought Michael liked to walk around with a fucking diaper-wearing monkey named Bubbles. Know what she said? "Because he's a genius." Having jellyfish makes me a genius because it keeps me from watching TV. I can learn more from watching fish swim in circles all day than watching Kim Kardashian talk about herself.

Another great thing that still has my head spinning was returning to *Saturday Night Live* on March 14, 2009—this time as the host. When you're a cast member, you have one point of view—you live and die by one, two, maybe three sketches a week. When you're the host, you have the pressure of the monologue and at least three or four sketches. I'd watched so many great people run through that routine during my seven years there. I always thought about what it would be like to host, and I most definitely dreamed about doing it one day.

None of those dreams were close to how it went down for me. The night I hosted, I was in *every single sketch*! That was a first in *SNL* history—no host before me had ever appeared in every sketch. I was even in the filmed sketch that was the introduction to the show. The only portions of the show I wasn't in were the musical numbers—and I would have shaken my ass or hit a tambourine with Kelly Clarkson if she'd asked me to.

It was a sweet victory for me to come back to *SNL* like that. I'd started out as "the black guy" on the show back in 1996. I was the lowest man on the totem pole and seen as a token by a lot of black comics. Over my years there I proved myself and became one of the top guys on the show, but to return and host the way I did was beyond great.

That night was the pinnacle for me—the best moment of my career so far. I felt like I was standing on the top of another mountain. I'd come back and hosted after being a cast member, and there are only twenty-five of us who have ever done that in thirty-four years! I'm up there with greats like Eddie Murphy, Chris Rock, Tina Fey, Bill Murray, Damon Wayans, Mike Myers, and Chevy Chase.

I broke down and cried when I got the call to come host; it came just after my Golden Globes speech, because, let's face it, they had to let me host after that. I had a dilemma though. After I got the call I was so excited that I called my son Tracy junior and told him right away. He told my ex-wife about it, and of course Sabina wanted to be there. To her it brought back old times, and she felt that since she was there for the struggles back in the day, she had to be there when I hosted—and I agreed. She was right, she'd been part of it. But things had changed, so I let my ex-wife and my kids come to the dress rehearsal and then let Taneisha come to the live show.

My first few days on set that week were very emotional, full of reminders of how far I'd come. I would stop in the hallways, and memories of my years living the show every week would rush back. I was so grateful just to be there I felt like hugging and thanking everyone involved whenever I saw them. I have to say once more: Marci! Marci Klein! You reading this, baby? I LOVE YOU! Marci was there that week, looking after me, making sure the show was running well and that I was happy. I just about tackled her whenever I saw her around the set. Anyway, after two or three days, I got control of myself and focused. My attitude was "Let's get to work! I want my show to be the bomb!" There was no more room for emotional shit. We had a show to do.

It was a very intense week. I wanted everything to be as professional and funny as it could possibly be, and I did my best to contribute all around. As the week progressed and we started to get those sketches up on the board, I realized that I was in all of them. It was amazing and a challenge that I was ready to tackle, but still I was worried about being able to bring my A game. I wanted to get all of my lines right; I wanted my timing and delivery to be perfect. I kept thinking about how many people had gone out of their way to make my show good for me. Tina Fey wrote my monologue, and that's why I love her, because she didn't have to do that. But she did, even though we had so much to do at *30 Rock* that week.

The night I hosted I gave it my all. I had to go a zillion miles per hour to do all of those costume changes between commercials, so my energy might not have been 100 percent the entire time. Also, *30 Rock* was wrapping up the season that week, so I'd come from shooting the show straight into *SNL* rehearsals at the real 30 Rock studios. All of that excitement and activity caused my blood pressure to rise, and when that happens to diabetics, they retain water. Midway through my rehearsal week at *SNL,* my legs swelled up badly. It's tough when that happens; I can't move naturally and my joints hurt. It's hard to bend my knees, and walking is uncomfortable. I'm just not myself on my feet—I almost fell down a flight of stairs the night of the show because I couldn't move normally.

My doctor estimated that I had about three gallons of extra water in each leg that week. He drained them twice with this big needle that he stuck in right above my knee. Every night Taneisha would put compresses on my legs and rub my feet, but my joints still ached. Each day between *30 Rock* and *SNL* rehearsals I went to my doctor's office to get my blood pressure and blood-sugar levels checked because he had me on several medicines that had to be monitored closely. My doctor even had to be there when I did the live show on Saturday because he was worried that I might have complications. But I got through it. You people know—you've read it all right here. It's never been easy—it's been through the roof since the day I was born.

I had a wonderful moment in my dressing room that night just before I went out and started the show. Taneisha and a few close friends were there. Alec Baldwin came in to wish me luck, my girl Tina Fey was there to make sure I was ready, and Lorne Michaels showed up too. Those rooms aren't big, and at that moment mine was filled with some important people in my life. I couldn't get emotional because we had a show to do, but somewhere in the back of my mind I took a little snapshot for my memory bank.

—

That was something, man. And what I've got coming is even better. I've learned a lot about myself, and there's one thing I can say for sure: I've come a long way and I've achieved a lot. I'm proud of that. But you know what? I'm not satisfied. I'm happy, I'm proud, but I'm not satisfied. I'll never be satisfied. Because I'm an artist and artists are always thinking of what they're going to do next and how to make that better than what they just did. I'm like Michael Jackson—I strive for perfection. Michael Jackson wasn't satisfied with "Billie Jean," and that is the greatest song ever written. But he didn't stop there; he kept going. And so will I.

I don't just want to strive for myself either. I always keep in mind that I can be an example to kids from backgrounds like mine. I hope that I continue to have an impact on young people and that I show them that hard work and dedication is the key to success. I also hope that the people who read my story find inspiration in it and understand that there is no simple path to follow. I have a God-given talent, but as I hope you've learned by reading about my life, that was not enough—it took hard work, perseverance, and luck. My path led to success, but the only guaranteed path in this world is to become educated and to work hard. That is not what I did, but I'm the exception, not the rule. The real answer is education, because knowledge is the key to the universe. Take it from me; I'm at the point in my life where I've realized that the best thing I can do for my career is to surround myself with people who are smarter than me. I do that as much as I can, every single day. And look at me—that shit is *working*.

Think about it this way: In basketball, everyone who played on a team with Michael Jordan put up their best numbers during those years of their career. It's true—you play with the best, you will be your best. That's why I play with Tina Fey; that's why I play with Chris Rock and Martin Lawrence. All of them make me better. I can get the job done, but when you have greatness on your team, you achieve your personal best.

I've only come to understand what it means to be a man over the last four years of my life. I'm fine with that, because I know plenty of motherfuckers who never get the memo on maturity. I look back and I regret hurting the people I've hurt and screwing up situations that weren't screwed up until I made them that way. But I can sleep at night knowing that even if I can't fix something, I've learned and I've grown. It wasn't that long ago that if someone pissed me off at ten in the morning, I'd be pissed off all day long. If it was a situation I couldn't change, I'd find someone else to be mad at, some other way to get that anger off my chest. These days if something doesn't go my way in the morning, by noon I have pulled myself together. My rule of thumb is that if I let myself get pissed off for 30 percent of my day but make sure 70 percent is still good, then I'm okay. A day that's 70 percent good should be enough to make anyone happy, it don't matter who you are. Those 100 percent days are rare and should be cherished. They're the gifts, not the norm.

I've been thinking about life and death more these days too. And the way I see it, that 70 percent rule applies there too. No one's perfect, and no one's got to know that more than the God who made us. Dude's got to figure that human beings do the best they can. The way I see it, if you're 70 percent good and fuck up 30 percent of your life, He will give you a pass. If your deeds are less than 70 percent good when you get to the pearly gates, I've got a feeling you won't be let in. I don't think 65 percent is gonna cut it. I think 65 means you're coming back and you're gonna clean some toilets and you're gonna shovel some shit. You won't have to do it with one hand or nothing too bad, but 65 ain't enough to walk right in and start enjoying the all-you-can-eat buffet. I look at it this way: I raised another man's children for twenty-one years. That's got to get me at least a good look from God, am I right? That has to be at least 50 of my 70 percent.

I'm not saying that I know this for sure, but I have a pretty good sense that these are good guidelines to follow. Living right isn't about being materialistic; it's not about being fit or looking good—it's personal and private, but it's something that all of us need to think about in this world. It has nothing to do with your religion, but it has everything to do with your relationship with God. Humans don't arrive on earth perfect; we have to work on ourselves—and no one is exempt from that duty. So keep this in mind next time you think about doing someone dirty. And keep this in mind next time you want to take your anger out on a stranger. You might not want to wreck your goodness grade-point average over some bullshit like that. Most important, none of us should ever judge another by what we see on the outside, because no one can ever really know what it's like to walk a mile in another person's shoes. I know this much: Plenty of people would cry if they walked a mile in mine. And plenty more would have fallen apart long ago with my boots on—but everything I've triumphed over just makes me smile wider these days.

I've lived, I've lost, I've survived, and I've strived. I'm a very lucky man; I've come through it all with scars and knowledge. I have done more than I ever dreamed I'd do, and I'm just getting started. I gave it my all, but like my dad said, life don't come with instructions. I had to learn all of this on my own, but I'll share some wisdom with you before I go: Be true to yourself and try your best to do no wrong.

I'm Tracy Morgan. Thank you for being here with me tonight. Now please go home!

ACKNOWLEDGMENTS

I'd like to thank Sabina and the kids, Taneisha Hall and her family, all my cousins and aunts, Leroy Williams, Gil, and my co-writer, Anthony Bozza, who was there with me through all of this, every step of the way. He and I shared some things, man. I want to thank Richard, who I love—we going to Benihana, Rich; that's where this whole thing started. My managers, my agents, and, most of all, I'd like to thank God. To all my relatives who are not here anymore, I love you. My man Spoon, Lorney Lorne Michaels, Tina Fey. Other people, if I missed you, you know I love you—*you know who you are*. Also my man Bradley Lewis, my man Corwin Moore, and my man Jonathan. And Kenny Pierce, the man, the myth. Kenny Pierce, you prick. And thank you to my man Joe, who takes care of my fish and my animals— I love you, Joe. And thank you Jonathan Smitty Banks. Also everybody at *30 Rock*. Jerry Cuffit. Marci Klein, I love you for giving me a shot on *SNL*. Thank you Barry Katz for believing in

ACKNOWLEDGMENTS

me, and Ms. Brown for letting me go when I first walked into a comedy club. Thank you my man Rock for inviting me to the workshop. Also Russell Simmons, Martin Lawrence, Eddie Murphy, Dick Gregory, Richard Pryor, Robin Harris, Sam Kinison, Jerry Seinfeld, Chris Rock, and all those comedians before me that paved the way. Lenny Bruce, thank you for taking the blows. And to all the young talent that's coming up behind me, keep on keeping up. To my sons, Malcolm, Tracy, and Gitrid, this one is for you, baby! Pull the trigger! All the youth out there, don't cheat yourself, treat yourself—good. Peace, I'm out.

Hold on, I got more. I also want to thank my doctors for keeping me alive and healthy: Dr. Lamb, Dr. Castellano, Dr. Weiss, and my other doctor, the female one who gave me my space boots. Thank you Mike Tadros, Bruce Willis, Kevin Smith—I love you. Neil LaBute, Clint Culpepper over at Screen Gems. Everybody that helped me with my career and my life. Thank you Brian Whale, a.k.a. Whale, all the OGs from Tompkins: Kito, Lenny, Ox, Twan, and my main man Allen. God bless the dead—rest in peace. I love you all. I'd also like to thank Michael Jackson and the Jackson family for all the inspiration they gave me to reach. Biggie Smalls too, and my man Puffy and all my friends in the music and entertainment industry who used to tell me I could do it. Biggie, rest in peace—thanks for telling me whenever you saw me, "Sky's the limit, baby. Sky's the limit." And before I end my acknowledgments I would like to acknowledge my grandfather Dave Warden and my grandma Rosalie Morgan. Grandma, Grandpa, I love you.

*All photographs within the text are copyright © 2009 by
Clay Patrick McBride. The photographs in the insert are
from the following sources:*

School picture of Tracy Morgan: courtesy of Tracy Morgan.
Picture of Tracy Morgan as a ring bearer: courtesy
    of Tracy Morgan.
Tracy Morgan family photos: courtesy of Tracy Morgan.
The *Clintonian* yearbook photos of Tracy Morgan: courtesy
    of DeWitt Clinton High School.
Photo of Tracy Morgan and Bert Blanco: courtesy of Bert Blanco.
Photo of Tracy Morgan in a football jersey during his visit back to
    DeWitt Clinton High School: courtesy of Bert Blanco.
Photo of Tracy Morgan surrounded by students: courtesy of
    Lawrence Lucier/Getty Images.
Stills from *Saturday Night Live* with Tracy as Maya Angelou,
    with Lorne Michaels, and with Yoda: courtesy of
    Mary Ellen Matthews/NBC Universal, Inc.

Photo from *The Tracy Morgan Show:* courtesy of NBC/Everett Collection.

Photo from *Crank Yankers:* courtesy of Scott Gries/Getty Images.

Still from *Saturday Night Live* with Tracy, Tina Fey, and Jimmy Fallon: courtesy of Mary Ellen Matthews/NBC Universal, Inc.

Still from *Saturday Night Live* with Tracy and Janet Jackson: courtesy of Dana Edelson/NBC Universal, Inc.

Photo from *The Longest Yard:* courtesy of Photofest.

Photo from *Little Man:* courtesy of Sony Pics/Everett/Rex Features.

Tracy with Alec Baldwin on the set of *30 Rock:* courtesy of Virgina Sherwood/NBC Universal, Inc.

Photo of Tracy as Tracy Jordan in the *30 Rock* pilot: courtesy of Eric Liebowitz/NBC Universal, Inc.

Tracy with Jane Krakowski and Lonny Ross: courtesy of Barbara Nitke/NBC Universal, Inc.

Photo of *30 Rock* cast members at the Screen Actors Guild Awards: courtesy of Frazer Harrison/Getty Images.

Photo of Tracy Morgan at the Golden Globes: courtesy of Paul Drinkwater/NBC Universal, Inc.

Photo of Tracy in *Big Love* skit on *SNL* in 2009: courtesy of Dana Edelson/NBC Universal, Inc.

Photo of Tracy and Sabina Morgan: courtesy of Scott Eells/Getty Images.

Photo of Tracy Morgan and family at the *Little Man* premiere: courtesy of Jeffrey Mayer/Getty Images.

AB OUT THE AUTHORS

ABOUT THE AUTHORS

TRACY MORGAN is an actor and a comedian. He was a cast member on *Saturday Night Live* for seven years, has had featured roles in numerous movies, and currently stars on the award-winning sitcom *30 Rock*. In 2009 he was nominated for an Emmy Award for his role as Tracy Jordan on that show. He lives in New York City.

ANTHONY BOZZA is a former *Rolling Stone* staff writer and the author of the #1 *New York Times* bestseller *Too Fat to Fish* with Artie Lange and the *New York Times* bestsellers *Whatever You Say I Am: The Life and Times of Eminem, Tommyland* with Tommy Lee, and *Slash* with Slash. He is also the publisher of Igniter, an imprint of HarperCollins. He lives in New York City and on the web at www.anthonybozza.net.

ABOUT THE TYPE

This book was set in Granjon, a modern recutting of a typeface produced under the direction of George W. Jones, who based Granjon's design upon the letter forms of Claude Garamond (1480–1561). The name was given to the typeface as a tribute to the typographic designer Robert Granjon.